*The Ideal of*
*Alexis de Tocqueville*

# The Ideal of Alexis de Tocqueville

### Manning Clark

*edited by*
Dymphna Clark
David Headon and
John Williams

**MELBOURNE UNIVERSITY PRESS**
IN ASSOCIATION WITH MANNING CLARK HOUSE

MELBOURNE UNIVERSITY PRESS
PO Box 278, Carlton South, Victoria 3053, Australia
info@mup.unimelb.edu.au
www.mup.com.au

Published in association with
MANNING CLARK HOUSE

First published 2000

Designed by Lauren Statham, Alice Graphics
Typeset by Syarikat Seng Teik Sdn Bhd, Malaysia
in 10/13 pt Trump Mediaeval and
10.5/13.5 pt Berkeley Book
Printed in Australia by Brown Prior Anderson

The National Library of Australia Cataloguing-in-Publication entry
for your forthcoming publication is as follows:

Clark, Manning, 1915–1991.
The ideal of Alexis de Tocqueville.
Bibliography.
Includes index.
ISBN 0 522 84925 3.

1. Tocqueville, Alexis de, 1805–1859. 2. Liberalism—France.
3. Politicians—France—Biography. 4. France—Politics and
government—19th century. 5. France—History—19th
century. I. Title.

944.007202

*Dedicated to the memory of*
*Dymphna Clark*
*18 December 1916 – 12 May 2000*
*An inspiration and example to all who knew her*

# Contents

# *Illustrations*

# Acknowledgements

Dymphna Clark gratefully acknowledges the enthusiasm and stamina of her co-editors, David Headon and John Williams, the instigators of this atypical enterprise. She also gives thanks to Teresa Pitt and the Melbourne University Press for their interest and faith in the project, to Brian Hubber, Rare Books Librarian of the State Library of Victoria, and to Faye Anderson, for finding and furnishing the key correspondence of Manning Clark and Professor R. M. Crawford.

All three editors owe deep thanks for the unending patience of Mary Walsh, Program Administrator of the Centre for Australian Cultural Studies (Canberra), who had to subdue an unruly text in two languages, with three sets of reference notes, two bibliographies and sundry other apparatus. Thanks also to Susan Cowan, Research Assistant in the School of Language, Literature and Communication, University College (ADFA), who read the manuscript at important stages, and to Professor Bruce Bennett, Head of the School, who continues to be a wonderful supporter of the cultural projects of the Centre for Australian Cultural Studies and Manning Clark House. In particular, the editors would like to acknowledge the contribution of this volume's Associate Editor, Sarah Randles, who worked on the manuscript with care when others might have succumbed to its complexities.

The Chronology and the Index are the work of Sebastian Clark; both reflect his usual diligence and acumen.

Finally, David Headon and John Williams would like to thank their partners, Billie and Wendy, for their constant support and generosity; they would also like to acknowledge the extraordinary energy and inspiration of their third editor.

# Editorial Notes

## Sources

The most obvious point to be made is that the published, manuscript and oral sources for Manning Clark's MA thesis on Tocqueville were limited entirely to material dating from before 1943, the year in which he wrote the work.

As far as printed material is concerned:

- During his time at Oxford, from October 1938 until late in 1939, he had at his disposal all the resources of the Bodleian Library.
- In July and August 1939 he paid several visits to the Bibliothèque Nationale in Paris.
- By 1943 his own collection already included a number of works on history (French, British and American), on literature and on political philosophy. The only work by Tocqueville which Clark himself then owned was a copy of the second edition (1856) of *L'Ancien Régime et la Révolution*, inscribed in his own hand: 'M. Clark—Balliol College—Oxford—14/11/1938'.
- Apart from notes taken from these three sources, in 1943 Clark spent as much time as possible—at weekends and in school holidays—at the Melbourne Public Library (now the State Library of Victoria), which fortunately held and still holds what appears to be the only full set in any library in Australia of the original 'Beaumont' edition (1868), of Tocqueville's *Oeuvres Complètes* (*OE.C.*).

On the basis of works consulted by Clark under these four headings, the bibliography at the end of the thesis lists ninety-nine printed works. Under the heading of *Unpublished Material at*

*Tocqueville*, Clark lists six categories. While there, he concentrated on reading as wide a range as possible of Tocqueville's (at that time) unpublished correspondence.

The most significant oral source tapped by Clark for this work was probably a discussion he had in Paris with Antoine Rédier, Tocqueville's biographer, in July 1939.

When reading Clark's thesis, it should be borne in mind that it was written in wartime without access to any sources except his own handwritten notes, compiled in Oxford and France in 1938 and 1939, and supplemented by occasional reference to the 1868 edition of Tocqueville's *Oeuvres Complètes*. There was little or no opportunity to check any of his material against other sources.

This edition attempts to correct any errors in Clark's citations, and silently corrects errors in the text itself. The small number of Clark's extended footnotes appearing in the body of the copy text has been retained, referred to using an asterisk. Additional footnotes provided by the editors are cited as 'a', 'b', 'c' etc.

## Copy Text

There were originally four typescript copies of the thesis. The 'top copy' was presumably submitted to Professor R. M. Crawford for examination. This copy can no longer be found. It may well have been sent by Professor Crawford in 1944 or 1945 to the publisher Victor Gollancz, in London, to be considered for publication (which never eventuated).

Of the three remaining copies, one was lodged with the library of the University of Melbourne, one was presented by Manning Clark to Dr and Mrs [Augustin] Lodewyckx (his parents-in-law), and one was retained by the author. For the editors of this volume the latter became the copy text, and it is the one to which we refer in our Introduction. It was the only copy to remain in Clark's hands, and in subsequent years was amended in a small number of significant ways. These amendments have been incorporated by the editors in this, the first edition of the thesis to be published.

## Translation from French

When translating the French used by Clark, the editors made the following decisions (to avoid disadvantaging in any way those readers with little or no knowledge of French):

- short French (or Latin) phrases commonly used in English (or recognisable by an English speaker) are left in italics;
- less common French phrases when used for the first time are followed by an English translation in square brackets; all subsequent use of the phrase consists only of the English translation, in quotation marks;
- more substantial French passages are, when not accompanied by a footnote, followed by an English translation in square brackets;
- when the French passage is footnoted by Clark, it is silently translated into English in the body of the thesis, and the French original moved to the footnote.

# Introduction

## Origins (Dymphna Clark)

MANNING'S DEEP INTEREST in Alexis de Tocqueville reaches back to his undergraduate days at the University of Melbourne. Tocqueville's name and the title at least of his most famous work, *De la Démocratie en Amérique*, must have cropped up in earlier subjects Manning studied in the very conventional course for the bachelor's degree in History and Political Science. Then, in 1937, a young Professor Max Crawford came as a *deus ex machina* and lifted Manning out of the doldrums of 'Establishment' history which had so disillusioned him. Crawford would certainly have discussed Tocqueville's views on the problems of liberty, equality and democracy in his 1938 course on the French Revolution. Manning, who as long as he lived was never able to conform, would have pricked up his ears at Tocqueville's talk of the 'tyranny of the majority'. Here was a historian who saw so much so clearly, felt so passionately about human liberty, yet was fated to watch impotently as all his hopes for liberal democracy in France crumbled before his eyes after 1848. Before Manning and I left Melbourne in August 1938, bound for Oxford and Bonn respectively, it was clearly understood that Manning would go to Balliol, where he would probably write a thesis on Tocqueville for an Oxford doctorate.

There were doubtless already echoes of Manning's ruminations on the subject in two fat black exercise books which he filled during his undergraduate years—mainly, perhaps, in 1936. He was under medical orders then not to study for examinations, and the black exercise books were labelled 'Jottings of a Recluse'. Alas, even after strenuous explorations in and under our house, these have not been found.

So we have to look at other sources to tell us about the origins and genesis of Manning's Master of Arts thesis on *The Ideal of Alexis de Tocqueville*. The most accessible is the account scattered throughout the early chapters of his autobiographical work *The Quest for Grace* (1990). The others are entries in his random diaries from 1940 to 1943, and letters written by Manning to Professor Crawford between 1938 and 1943.

When Manning finally arrived in Oxford in the autumn of 1938, the whole picture changed: it became plain that his slender Bartlett Scholarship of £100 per year was hopelessly inadequate for the three years required for an Oxford doctorate. Nor was he attracted to the very narrow research requirements for that degree. Instead, without consulting his Melbourne mentors, he plunged enthusiastically into an advanced course on European History of the nineteenth century, under the general supervision of his revered Balliol tutor Humphrey Sumner. In Manning's mind:

> The only argument against this [decision] was that, in this course, I would not be actually taking out a degree and that may jeopardize my chances for a job in the future. But I came to the conclusion that the benefit which I would obtain from such a course would ultimately outweigh the immediate bargaining power of an Oxford degree.
> (Clark to Crawford, Crawford Papers—Balliol College, Oxford, 24.1.39)[1]

---

[1] This and following dated quotations are from letters from Manning Clark to Professor R. M. Crawford, Crawford Papers, University of Melbourne Archives.

The University authorities in Melbourne were not pleased. Under pressure, Manning enrolled for a B.Litt. degree after all. This would take two years and require exhaustive research on a very minor topic. To allay some of the misgivings in Melbourne, Manning then announced that his financial troubles were over: Balliol had asked him to teach some of their overseas students, and in any case 'married life in Oxford is much cheaper than single life' (16.3.39). We were married at the end of January 1939.

In this and other letters to Crawford, Manning frequently asks about his prospects of university work or a research grant when he returns to Australia. Two other themes reappear regularly: firstly, his immense gratitude to Max Crawford himself: 'It would not be untrue to say that without your inspiration and instruction I would never have had the opportunity' (24.1.39); and, secondly, his quickened interest in the history of Australia: 'The experience here has fired me with enthusiasm . . . I do feel that I can do something with the Australian material and am certain that there is a lot to be done to correct the impression left by Turner, Ruskin [Rusden] etc.' (16.3.39).

Three months later, his course is finally set. He reports to Crawford:

> When I returned to Oxford for the summer term, I wanted to write a thesis on English opinion of the Anglo-Russian Entente of 1907–14. Mr Sumner persuaded me to drop the idea and concentrate on more familiar ground. He suggested that I should write a thesis on Alexis de Tocqueville—an expansion of an idea which I had presented to him in an essay on de Tocqueville. So I sent in my application . . . and within a week I had the permission of the Board to write a thesis on the Political and Social Ideas of A. de Tocqueville, with Mr Sumner as supervisor. I began collecting material soon after the term began . . . So far I have read all the secondary printed material . . . and have begun to read the *Oeuvres Complètes*.
> (19.6.39).

That summer Manning and I spent three weeks working on the mass of unpublished material in the family archives in the *Chartrier* of the Château of Tocqueville in Normandy. Humphrey Sumner had arranged for us to be admitted to that Holy of Holies, but the then Comte looked rather askance at this harum-scarum couple. Was *this* a gentleman scholar from Oxford? With a young wife, so obviously *enceinte*? Not really *comme il faut*, either of them ... We were quickly told that the Count's *cuisinière* was *malade*. She remained indisposed during the whole of our stay.

But we were made warmly welcome as paying guests in the much smaller château of Madame la Baronne de Resbecq in nearby Cosqueville. A rickety autorail conveyed us each day through the Normandy countryside between the two villages.

During that summer of 1939 the political clouds gathered fast over Europe. On 28 August both Tocqueville and Cosqueville were plastered with posters announcing the mobilisation of the French army. World War II was just six days away. M. le Comte immediately informed us that the *Chartrier* at Tocqueville was no longer open to us. We had to pack our bags and cross the channel from Cherbourg, back to Oxford.

That was virtually the end of Manning's original research on Tocqueville, for the war soon closed in on Oxford. The foreign students Manning had taught for Balliol all evaporated, leaving him almost penniless. Through Sumner's influence, Manning became Senior History Master at Blundell's School (of *Lorna Doone* fame) in Tiverton, Devon. The headmaster, Neville Gorton (later the inspired Anglican Bishop of war-torn Coventry), immensely stimulated Manning as a teacher and remained a lifelong influence. Manning wrote to Crawford:

> The standard of the History Sixth is the same as 2nd year at the Melbourne University. The better boys read Troeltsch, Gason etc.
> (Blundell's School, Tiverton, 24.12.39)

And again, a few week later: 'But—and it is a big but—I am almost like a child in my enthusiasm and desire to have something to do with Australian education' (14.1.40).

In the same letter he continues:

> My work on Tocqueville is assuming definite shape … So far
> I have finished the work on Tocqueville himself, and also the
> political philosophers of his time, Constant, Guizot, Royer-
> Collard & Thiers. I have also done a lot of work on the Rev-
> olution of 1848, particularly the pamphlets published at the
> time, which Tocqueville himself had collected—by Lamennais,
> Blanqui and Babet [Barbès]. This term, in the intervals between
> school-teaching, I hope to read Marx on 1848—the *Poverty of
> Philosophy* (in which he criticised Tocqueville by implication).

Then follows a catalogue of other historians he plans to read:
Mignet, Taine, Michelet etc.; of the relevant German writers,
beginning with Heine; of French and German social and political novelists; and of writers like Montesquieu, Rousseau,
Locke, Bonald and de Maistre whom he will re-read 'to fill in
the background'. He concludes:

> I had planned to write the thesis in the summer vacation but at
> Tiverton it is difficult to get hold of books.
> (14.1.40)

Whatever 'definite shape' Manning's thesis—'Toccers'—had
assumed by January 1940, the gestation was to take four more
long years.

The English spring and summer of 1940 were particularly
bright and beautiful. Manning continued to take his History
Sixth to Exeter each Wednesday to practise research in the
town archives. On Saturdays he took his victorious cricket XI
to matches at Downside, Taunton and other gentlemanly
cricket grounds. But the war drew closer daily. By night the
German bombers flew overhead on their way to Bristol, and
the History Sixth shrank daily as the older boys enlisted one
by one. Manning was unfit for military service.

In early July we three—Manning, our seven-month-old
Sebastian and I—sailed from Southampton for Australia on
the beautiful ship *Orcades*. There were jutting wrecks of
bombed allied ships to both port and starboard as we steamed

up the harbour of Gibraltar, and when our ship disembarked a whole troop of British marines there, we realised we were a perfectly legitimate military target. From Gibraltar the *Orcades* struck well south to the freezing forties to avoid raiders and minefields. At every alert—and there were many —Manning clutched first his son, then the old briefcase holding his 'Toccers' notes, before he glanced around for other baggage. On 10 August we docked at Port Melbourne and were gathered in as from the brink of the grave by our people. The talk in the town was largely of the outrageous plans to introduce petrol rationing in Australia.

*Sans* Oxford degree there was indeed no job for Manning at any university and no research money for the work on Tocqueville. In September 1940 James (later Sir James) Darling gave him a job and he became acting Senior History Master at Geelong Grammar School, Corio. His success with the boys of the History Sixth and the prowess of the cricket XI he coached were not enough to reconcile him to his own malaise in the Establishment environment of Corio. Manning quickly decided that his only escape route was via a higher degree, and the Tocqueville thesis hung like a chimera over our next three years.

In spite of his plea to be allowed time to write his thesis, the Victorian Education Department insisted that he study for the Bachelor of Education degree. Manning's anger spilled over into a letter to Professor Crawford:

> . . . as you know I am very anxious to produce a work on Tocqueville in the course of this year and I was anxious to find a means which would allow me to devote my whole time to it. But this was not to be and now the little time left after teaching will be absorbed by the wretched course for the Education Dept. So I feel at a dead end—and bitter but not down. I know what I want and shall find the means somehow, or bust in the endeavour. The alternative is a very grim one—the most ruthless and soul-destroying exploitation in return for a social position which has neither appeal nor value . . . In the meantime I am working on the Tocqueville. I am just beginning to re-read the classical works on political philosophy—Plato, Aristotle, Machiavelli,

Hobbes and Locke. I am hoping to do an article on Australian
culture soon ...
(Corio, 10.3.41)

At the end of the year Manning sat for two of the B.Ed. subjects. The result was two curt N's on his Academic Record.[2]
Eventually he escaped through a bureaucratic loophole by
sitting ('With a roomful of 14-year-olds') and passing the
examination for the Teacher's Primary Training Certificate.
These blots on his educational escutcheon did not prevent a
session of the Faculty of Education of the University of Melbourne from passing a special vote of thanks for his outstanding contributions to Victorian education when he departed
for Canberra in 1949.

The details of Manning's enrolment for the Melbourne
Master of Arts degree are not documented. It was presumably
some time in 1942 (the letter is not dated) that he wrote to
Professor Crawford:

Dear Sir, I learnt yesterday ... that the Australian [Common-
wealth] Literary Fund would not give me a research grant ... It
means that I must stay here another year—In the meantime I
have been working hard at the Tocqueville ... One great gap is
the lack of people to talk to about the subject. I wonder whether
you could spare the time in the future for such a conversation.
I realise that you must be very busy and that such a conversation can be of little value to you. But one can get very off the
track without the discipline of external criticism.

Yours sincerely

Manning Clark
Geelong Grammar School (nd)

One must assume that there was no supervision whatsoever
of Manning's work. Professor Crawford himself was absent
from Australia from November 1942 until December 1943,
while he served as First Secretary to the Australian Delegation

---

[2] Manning Clark File, University of Melbourne Archives (hereafter, Clark
File).

to the Soviet Union, and there were doubtless other wartime difficulties. This letter is the last communication we have between Manning and Crawford for four years. The correspondence—still full of gratitude and respect on Manning's part—is resumed in 1946 when Crawford entrusted to him the teaching of the course on Australian History at the University of Melbourne.

Apart from his own notes, collected in Oxford and Tocqueville in 1939, there were no resources to support Manning's work on the thesis except very occasional visits to the Melbourne Public Library (State Library of Victoria). Here at least he had an extraordinary stroke of luck: this was—and still is, I understand—the only library in Australia holding a complete set of Tocqueville's *Oeuvres Complètes* in the original 1868 edition edited by Tocqueville's close friend, Gustave de Beaumont. Manning himself owned only one work by Tocqueville, a copy of *L'Ancien Régime et la Révolution* in the second 1856 edition, inscribed 'M. Clark—Balliol College—Oxford 14/11/38'. Given the scant time he could devote to writing and the almost total inaccessibility of source material, he may surely be excused the odd lapse in transcription and other minor errors.

We can trace the halting progress of the Tocqueville thesis through entries in Manning's random diaries. Most are full of self-castigation, self-doubt and despair. Some of them reflect the depth of Manning's preoccupation—not to say identification—with Tocqueville's personality and *angoisses*. Here are a few of the entries:

5.5.1940
> I would like to do two things, to write a good novel ... Then I want to write a biography of de Tocqueville, wh. would give me a reputation—I suspect my motives here, as satisfaction of my ambition ...[3] (Blundell's, Devonshire)

---

[3] Papers of C. M. H. Clark, National Library of Australia (hereafter, Clark Papers).

20.9.42

... a bad day on the Tocqueville—only one page & that
included two long quotations. I am aware of the gulf bet. the
gt. ideas in my mind and the poverty of what I put down.[4] I
console myself by saying that the first draft is an attempt to
find out what I think ... But I have no 'leit motiv' ... How
lazy I am! (Geelong Grammar School, Corio)

26.9.42

Failed with the Toc.—9 lines, very poor in quality. More
determined than ever to be a writer, but still doubt my
powers—I have wasted my life ... I think men who write are
types who cannot satisfy their craving for being noticed
except by writing ...[5]

29.9.42

Not an idea in my head—last night my mind was teeming
with them.

18.10.42

Could not do anything with the Tocqueville ... spent the day
in idle fantasies[6] ... life here is so meaningless ...

Early in December 1942 Manning starts to pull himself
together—there has to be a new start:

6.12.42

I have begun to think about the Tocqueville again. By now
the impressions and ideas stimulated during the first reading
of the material have become less strong ... even dim. I think
too that I have lost the desire to prove a case, to achieve
recognition ... So I must find a method of re-kindling my
enthusiasm and interest. What I mean is: the writing of the

---

[4] Cf. letter from Tocqueville to Mme Swetchine, 26.2.1857, quoted in
A. Rédier, *Comme disait Monsieur de Tocqueville*, pp. 282–3; Tocque-
ville's correspondence with Mme Swetchine in Alexis de Tocqueville,
*Oeuvres Complètes (1951– )*, hereafter, *OE.C.*, XV, 2.

[5] Cf. Rédier, *Tocqueville*, p. 283; J. P. Mayer, *Prophet of the Mass Age*,
p. 143.

[6] Rédier, *Tocqueville*, p. 283; Mayer, *Prophet of the Mass Age*, p. 143.

Tocqueville was a phantasy [*sic*] for me—I dreamt of it[7] . . . so much that I dissipated the original energy—now I must also start again. Fortunately I still have the material . . .

7.12.42

What myths did Toc. conceive or use to make his life bearable? . . . the myth of the perfect life in the Ancien Régime. It was this wh. made him ignore the shocking conditions of life for the servants of the nobility, wh. made him notice only the relationship and not the poverty of the servant—I think too the references to an 'ideal world in wh. my spirit loves to dwell'[8] is connected with this myth—he took comfort from contemplation of such a world.

15.12.42

I believe that my ideas are more mature and more likely to withstand a critical examination, but the ease of phrase . . . has disappeared—I have lost confidence, or rather the bubble of my conceit has been pricked . . .

16.12.42

. . . an idle day . . .

Suddenly, on Christmas Eve of 1942, the diary entry becomes a mass of criss-crossed notes, points, themes and questions spread over five pages:

24.12.42

. . . am exhausted by the day's work . . . Have I read my evidence too hastily? . . . why the violence in 1848? Why not peaceful development? Why this cataclysm? . . . Who is to blame? . . . The élite believe in liberty, the higher pleasures of the spirit—masses are not interested in them . . . So far only one point—Toc as example of weakness in liberal creed— methods he suggested did not realise the desired end— instead the reverse.

And finally, a big question, which is also our question:

What is value of knowing Toc? Is he important today?

---

[7] Cf. Rédier, *Tocqueville*, p. 282.
[8] Ibid.

On Christmas Day and again on 29 December 1942 the diary records many more 'Random Thoughts on Tocqueville'. Then there is total silence on the subject for almost a year. On 6 December 1943 Manning records:

Today I finished checking the manuscript of *The Ideal of Alexis de Tocqueville*. It is pleasant to have finished it. But I feel no elation, mainly because I am not satisfied with the performance.

Then immediately, on the same page, he admonishes himself:

Note the following lessons:
(I) Always write down ideas in a literary form wh. impressions from reading are still fresh.
(ii) ......
(vii) Eliminate the vulgarities, the elliptical phrases.
(viii) Improve vocabulary.[9]

I typed the thesis at night on an old secondhand typewriter, producing a top copy and three carbon copies. The typing was less than professional and the binding very rudimentary. I could wish now that I had been better versed in the Tocqueville world myself to mitigate 'the lack of people to talk to about the subject'. With three not very ruly children under four and few conveniences, there was not much time for 'the higher pleasures'.

The thesis was submitted, examined (history does not relate by whom) and awarded first class honours. Manning was dubbed Master of Arts in the old Wilson Hall on 5 September 1944. Professor Crawford referred twice to the thesis in official correspondence: first when he wrote to Manning's father to apologise for not attending the graduation ceremony —'Your son was awarded his Master of Arts for an excellent piece of work which I am encouraging him to publish'—and again in a letter to the Vice-Chancellor, whom he informed that he was 'in touch with Mr Victor Gollancz about the publication of Clark's thesis'. He went on: 'I believe he has the makings of a very distinguished historian' (Crawford Papers).

---

[9] Diary, Clark Papers.

It must have been at this time, when publication was in the air, that I was asked to insert into our copy of the thesis interlinear translations of the long quotations in French. They are still there, but the ink has faded and the pages have yellowed. The negotiations with the publisher must have petered out—it was still wartime.

It is indeed strange that this firstling from Manning's pen should now, so many years later, at last see the light of day. Yet the thesis serves still as a Tocqueville primer for Australians.

## Tocqueville and Australia

'WHAT IS VALUE of knowing Toc? Is he important today?' Manning Clark wrote in his diary on Christmas Eve 1942, and we must ask this question again fifty-eight years later. In particular, is he important for Australia?

Interest in Tocqueville, so universally revered in his own time and until the end of his century, lapsed in the first quarter of the twentieth century. '*On l'oublia*'—he was forgotten—wrote Antoine Rédier, whose book *Comme disait M. de Tocqueville*, published in 1925, marked the beginning of a new wave of interest. This has since swelled into a flood. There were at least three editions of Rédier's book in its first year. Dozens of volumes of learned commentary on Tocqueville and his thought now crowd the shelves of our university libraries, although one may search in vain for a complete set of his own works. The University of Toronto Press issues a regular *Tocqueville Review/Revue Tocqueville* (text in English and French). In 1997 a television series on Tocqueville was shown in North America. Granted that American citizens have their own obvious reasons to study his work, how can we explain this torrent of interest? If the serious reading public and the educators of Europe and America are so convinced of his relevance today, perhaps we in Australia should also look at what Tocqueville had to say about the big issues of Western society—about liberty, equality and democracy, and the compatibility of all three.

It may come as a surprise to learn that Tocqueville also wrote at length on the Australian colonies of his time. The official reason for his visit to America (which inspired his most famous work *De la Démocratie en Amérique*) was to examine the penal system of the United States and the new penitentiaries being established there. In this context Tocqueville made a detailed comparative study of the transportation of convicted prisoners to the Australian colonies and published a report of some 10 000 words on the Australian penal colonies as an appendix to *Du Système pénitentiaire aux Etats-Unis* (1833) and another almost as long in the introduction to the second edition of the same work.[10]

Tocqueville himself never visited Australia and his accounts are based almost exclusively on official documents such as the *Bigge Report* (1822), the *House of Commons Report on Secondary Punishments* (1832) and the official correspondence of Lord Bathurst with Bigge (1819) and with Governor Bourke (1834). He also repeated some of the (not always reliable) observations of his friend and compatriot E. de Blosseville in his *Histoire des Colonies Pénales de l'Angleterre dans l'Australie* (1831).

Tocqueville's observations on Australia do not make dull reading—they are too strongly partisan for that. He and his friend and collaborator Gustave de Beaumont were (unlike Blosseville) fierce supporters of the new penitentiary system of penology, as opposed to the deportation system on which the Australian colonies were founded. This emphasis is very marked.

Tocqueville's personal preoccupations emerge clearly in his judgements on the colonies of New South Wales and Van Diemen's Land, when compared with the early Puritan colonies of North America. In one passage we find this brief eulogy of the old colonies of American New England:

A handful of sectarians land on the shores of North America at the beginning of the seventeenth century. There, almost in secret, they found a society based on liberty and religion. This

---

[10] Alexis de Tocqueville: *Ecrits sur le système pénitentiaire en France et à l'Etranger, O.C.*, IV, 1, pp. 97–107, 269–80.

band of pious adventurers has since become a great people, and the nation they have created has remained the freest and the strongest in the faith in the whole world.[11]

In contrast to these paragons of North America:

> ... of all British colonies, Australia is the only one deprived of those precious civil liberties which constitute the glory of England and the strength of its offshoots in all parts of the world. How could men who themselves but recently stood trial before the Court of Assizes be entrusted with the functions of a jury? And how can public business be safely handed over to a populace plagued by its own vices and riven by deep hostilities?[12]

While these sentiments on Britain's transportation system would hardly have been popular in Australia, either with its ruling military elite or with its convict class and emancipists in the deeply self-conscious 1830s, Tocqueville was destined to emerge as a significant and respected voice in the self-government debates of the 1850s. The man primarily responsible for this curious outcome was outspoken Australian Briton William Charles Wentworth.

Wentworth was an enigmatic man. The darling of the native-born New South Wales population in the 1820s—due to his central role in the establishment of freedom of the press and his celebrated encounters with Governor Ralph Darling —by the 1840s his status and reputation amongst the same group had deteriorated to the point that he was denounced in Sydney's popular press as frothing 'like a rabid bulldog'.[13] What had happened in the intervening years to cause such a sudden fall from grace? First of all, Wentworth's material circumstances changed dramatically after his father's death in 1827 resulting in a substantial inheritance. Shrewd acqui-

---

[11] Tocqueville, *Système pénitentiaire*, p. 278.
[12] Ibid., p. 280. A careful study and summary of Tocqueville's observations and reflections on the Australian colonies is included in Colin Forster: *France and Botany Bay*, pp. 92–117.
[13] See C. M. H. Clark, *A History of Australia*, vol. II, p. 245.

sition of many large properties in New South Wales followed; in turn, Wentworth began to defend the emergent squattocracy against the claims of a rising tide of immigrants and native-born agitating for more land. The 'people' became, for Wentworth, a mob of 'dirty ruffians' who, for the well-being of the colony, had to be excluded from all branches of executive power on the basis of property, experience and education.[14]

This was the stance Wentworth took into 1853 as the inhabitants of the colony of New South Wales began to debate in earnest their draft Constitution Bill. It was a political position certain to encounter opposition. Indeed, Wentworth's antagonists gathered together, in Sydney's Victoria Theatre on 16 August 1853, to express their disgust with his commitment to a hereditary peerage system. Chief among these was the young currency lad Daniel Henry Deniehy who, in a speech destined to take its place among Australian political history's finest, denounced Wentworth's intended class of local lords as nothing but 'bunyip' aristocrats, aspiring 'political oligarchs' who 'treated the people at large as if they were cattle to be bought and sold in the market'.[15] If New South Wales was to have an aristocracy, Deniehy proclaimed, let it not resemble 'that of William the Bastard but of Jack the Strapper'.

During this speech, amidst the constant laughter and applause of the crowd, Deniehy questioned the credentials of several well-known members of the local landed gentry. He ridiculed them all, but it was at Wentworth that he directed his most stinging criticism. Deniehy publicly questioned Wentworth's patriotism, his motivations and, above all, the dubious moral stature of his life in politics. Furious at this vilification, Wentworth the very next day delivered a long speech in the Legislative Council—concluding the debate on the second reading of the Constitution Bill—in which he sought to justify his position through aggressive denunciation

---

14 Quoted in A. C. V. Melbourne, *William Charles Wentworth*, p. 55.
15 Daniel Henry Deniehy, ' "Bunyip Aristocracy" Speech', in D. Headon and E. Perkins, eds, *Our First Republicans*, pp. 128–30.

of those he labelled the movement 'out of doors', the 'wild democrats', 'the dirty ruffians' and 'anarchists'.[16] The terms of Wentworth's defence make for compelling reading for, despite his much-quoted assertion that he wanted 'a British, not a Yankee Constitution', and that he 'heartily despise[d]' the 'American model', the overwhelming number of his scholarly and political references is either to Americans or to documents referring to America.[17] These include George Washington, Alexander Hamilton, John Calhoun, Alexis de Tocqueville and the 1852 *American Almanac*. Each is cited with obvious confidence in the reception of its authority. One source, however, dominates: the Frenchman Tocqueville, and his seminal publication *Democracy in America*.

Though Tocqueville would not have approved of Wentworth's manipulative selections from his work, he would have been flattered by the sheer extent of the homage. In Wentworth's Constitution Bill speech, occupying some fifty-four columns of newspaper reportage, approximately thirty-one focus on American federal and constitutional issues, the majority of this content consisting of verbatim sections from *Democracy in America*.[18] Wentworth advocated government action to favour the 'great interests' of the country in rural electoral districts and to fortify the Legislative Council against the incursions of popular opinion through a colonial peerage. The 'very celebrated' *Democracy in America* is the central reference point in all nine of Wentworth's assertions about democracy's effect on the 'social condition of the people of America'.[19] However, at opportune moments he deliberately shifts from a Tocqueville excerpt to his own paraphrasing, reconstituting the French writer for his own political purposes. Wentworth asserts that democracy 'excludes from power the upper and best educated classes' and 'throws the government . . . into the hands of the lower classes'; it dis-

---

[16] E. Silvester, ed., *New South Wales Constitution Bill*, pp. 25, 34, 38.
[17] Silvester, *New South Wales Constitution Bill*, pp. 35, 51.
[18] See N. D. McLachlan, ' "The Future America": Some Bicentennial Reflections', p. 380.
[19] Silvester, *New South Wales Constitution Bill*, p. 40.

courages society's most talented individuals from entering politics, resulting in public offices being 'for the most part filled with corrupt and incompetent functionaries'; and it encourages 'revolting scenes' in its state legislatures, where 'the bowie knife and revolver are frequently resorted to . . . with deadly effect'.[20]

Wentworth develops his case to damn democracy around selective Tocquevillean argument for two reasons: the Frenchman's prestige as a commentator on democracy and the fact that, according to Wentworth, Tocqueville, 'so deeply . . . imbued with democratic prejudices', could nonetheless condemn the American example as a 'degrading' tyranny.[21] In using Tocqueville in this way, Wentworth applied him to the Australian situation exactly as Sir Robert Peel cited the Frenchman in Britain to lay 'the foundations of the great party of conservative resistance, after the popular movement of 1832'.[22] Peel posited *Democracy in America* as a Tory book, quoting extensively from it in 1835 during the Commons debate on election bribery, and again in 1837 in his inaugural address as Lord Rector of the University of Glasgow.[23] Predictably, he highlighted the sections on the tyranny of the majority. With the shouts of the Victoria Theatre mob ringing in his ears, in 1853 Australia, William Charles Wentworth would do exactly the same.

In the decades following the self-government debates of the 1850s, Tocqueville disappears from colonial view. Gold, 'marvellous' Melbourne, ambition and political bunching shape an era when Tocqueville was probably perceived as an irrelevance. What is surprising, however, is that he fails to re-emerge at the historical moment when one might have expected his influence to be at its keenest: the Federation debates of the 1890s. The framers of the Australian Constitution, when casting around for constitutional inspiration,

---

[20] Ibid., pp. 40–8.
[21] Ibid., p. 49.
[22] See D. P. Crook, *American Democracy in English Politics: 1815–1850*, p. 176.
[23] Ibid., p. 191.

looked to a number of federal systems. The United States, the Swiss and the Canadian models all offered insights into the operation of this challenging form of governance. While the United States proved to be an inspiration to many Australian colonists, its understanding was sought only from familiar teachers. For instance, when the framers of the Australian Constitution searched for accounts of America and its institutions it was not to Montesquieu or Tocqueville that they turned. As Sir Samuel Griffith noted during the 1891 National Australasian Convention in Sydney when discussing the separation of powers:

> The origins of this difference [between the United States and the United Kingdom] lie in the fact that the framers of the American Constitution had been frightened by the tendency then lately exhibited in the United Kingdom of ministers to overawe Parliament, and they thought it extremely desirable to separate the executive and legislative branches of government, following the arguments of a great writer—I should rather say a celebrated writer—of those days, Montesquieu, the wisdom of whose observations and the accuracy of whose deductions and assumption of principles may be, I submit with great respect, very open to doubt.[24]

The once 'great' Montesquieu was now merely 'celebrated' and, in the mind of Griffith and others, a little suspect. So too, when discussing America it was not Tocqueville's *Democracy in America* that caught their interest. Rather, it was James Bryce's *The American Commonwealth* (1888) that took on the burden of guide.

There are many reasons why Bryce's work and not Tocqueville's was elevated to the status of constitutional 'Bible'.[25] The first was its appearance at the precise moment when Federation was again being contemplated.[26] Alfred Deakin, who

---

[24] *Official Report of the National Australasian Convention Debates*, p. 35.
[25] J. A. La Nauze, *The Making of the Australian Constitution*, p. 273.
[26] The first edition was published in 1888, the second in 1891, the third in 1895 and the fourth in 1910.

*Two young Australians en route for 'Europe, the land of holy wonders'*
*Dymphna, Naples, August 1938*
*Manning on board SS Orama, August 1938*

*'Am Rhein, dem heiligen Strome' (on the Rhine, the holy stream)—Manning at Godesberg, January 1939*

*Manning (back row, second from left) and fellow members of
Balliol touring cricket team, summer 1939*

*Manning and two distinguished
members of the Balliol touring
cricket team: Tim (later Sir
Timothy) Bligh and Professor
Henry Whitehead (wearing a
Harlequins cap)*

*Manning ruminates at Tocqueville, Normandy, August 1939*

*Aspirant and mentor? Manning at the foot of the bust of Alexis de Tocqueville, Tocqueville, Normandy, August 1939*

*Coffee and* cassis *on the terrace after Sunday lunch, with Madame la Baronne de Resbecq (front left) and several paying and non-paying guests, Cosqueville, Normandy, August 1939. Manning and Dymphna are at rear, left*

*Manning with 'le petit Yvan qui est si gai'—Ivan, the youngest
son of Madame la Baronne de Resbecq, Cosqueville, August 1939*

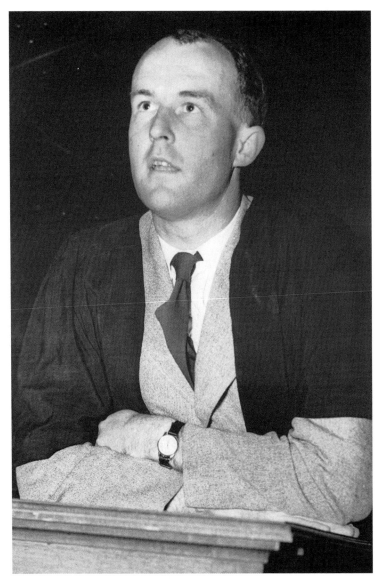

*The fired-up young lecturer at the University of Melbourne, 1944*

*The apprentice historian in his study at Croydon, Victoria, 1945*

*The home of Manning and Dymphna, 1945–1950, in Croydon*

introduced the work to many delegates, had made personal contact with Bryce in London in 1887 as part of a delegation to the Imperial Conference.[27] Bryce assumed another familiarity for the framers. He was after all British, the Member for Aberdeen, and legally qualified—as the Regius Professor of Civil Law at Oxford. Also, his work contained examples from the English experience.[28] However, there was one critical factor which ensured that Bryce would strike a chord with many of the Australian framers—namely, as James Warden notes, the fact that Bryce eschewed theory.[29]

In the introduction to his work, Bryce states that while it may have seemed 'natural' for him to 'tread in the steps' of Tocqueville, he rejected that path. He states that what Tocqueville has 'given us is not so much a description of the country and people as a treatise'.[30] Bryce, on the other hand, assures his readers that he has

> . . . striven to avoid the temptation of the deductive method, and to present simply the facts of the case, arranging and connecting them as best I can, but letting them speak for themselves rather than pressing upon the reader my own conclusion.[31]

For Australia's Federation fathers, Bryce was an accessible source. His lack of theoretical clutter appealed to many of the Australian framers, who congratulated themselves on their practical temperament. They found Tocqueville a little intimidating, and a bit too foreign.

Tocqueville scholarship in Australia since Federation has been at best sporadic, the long silences broken only by occasional commentary on the French historian's writings on penology. Had 'The Ideal of Alexis de Tocqueville' been published by Victor Gollancz, as Max Crawford hoped it might in

---

[27] Deakin had travelled to the Imperial Conference in London in 1887. See Alfred Deakin, *The Federal Story: The Inner History of the Federal Cause 1880–1900*, pp. 19–25.

[28] For instance, his examples such as value of goods or salary always contain the conversion of dollars into pounds.

[29] See J. Warden, 'Federalism and the Design of the Australian Constitution'.

[30] J. Bryce, *The American Commonwealth*, vol. I, pp. 4–5.

[31] Ibid., p. 5.

August 1945,[32] it could have been a different story. The thesis was not published, and Tocqueville remained a footnote to Australia's Old World connections.

## Manning Clark and Tocqueville's Ideal

THE PUBLICATION AT LAST OF Manning Clark's *The Ideal of Alexis de Tocqueville* is both disconcerting and a relief. It is disconcerting in that the work appears almost a decade after his death when in fact it represents the first major step in his remarkable academic career. In perusing the work the reader is constantly struck by 'Clarkesque' phrases and methods which were to become as familiar as his goatee beard and dark, broad-brimmed hat. Yet these are the embryonic thoughts of a young man in his twenties, a scholar who had yet to familiarise himself fully with a historical apparatus through which he was to build a body of work. The *Ideal* is also a relief in that it provides answers to questions about Clark and his approach to history. Just as Clark often repeats Dostoevsky's wish, 'I want to be there when everyone suddenly understands what it has all been for', the work provides a catalyst for ideas and explanations from which Clark was to drink deeply throughout his career. Indeed, it is in this work that Dostoevsky first appears.

The feature that must be noted when reading the thesis is its timing. From the preface to the conclusion, the spectre of war and Nazism loomed over the author's pen. As Clark himself notes, quoting W. H. Auden: 'The lights of the "low, dishonest decade" were flickering fitfully'.[33] Like Auden, Clark is writing of a time when 'Fortune has pedalled furiously away'.[34] Indeed, Clark is well aware of the privilege, and even delusion, he and his fellow researchers experienced in the

---

[32] Letter from Prof. R. M. Crawford to the Vice-Chancellor, University of Melbourne, 21 August 1945, Crawford Papers.

[33] W. H. Auden, *Collected Shorter Poems 1930–1944*, Preface, p. 1. The poem quoted is '1st September 1939'.

[34] Ibid., 'In War Time'.

vaults of the Bodleian Library at Oxford. 'Lost . . . in history'[35] they would have wished to remain. However, the events outside Oxford disturbed that wish. As he tries to understand the failures of Tocqueville, Clark is clearly addressing the circumstances in which the world found itself in 1943. How is it, asks Clark, that the ideal propounded by Tocqueville had left the world infested by 'poverty, anarchy and war'? Clark can only come to some understanding of this conundrum by first engaging in an exploration of the man and the ideal.

Before dealing with the substance of Clark's argument concerning Tocqueville, however, it is worth recalling the basic details of the Frenchman's life. He was born in Paris on 29 July 1805 into an aristocratic Normandy family.[36] The third child of Hervé de Tocqueville and Louise Le Peletier de Rosanbo, he inherited from his parents the family traits of a 'deep rooted Catholic Christianity and aristocratic pride and dignity'.[37] He studied law in Paris (1823–26) and then was appointed an assistant magistrate at Versailles (1827). After the July 1830 Revolution he was demoted to a minor judicial position. In 1831 Tocqueville, with his friend Gustave de Beaumont, set sail for New York ostensibly to conduct a study of the American penal system. Upon their return to France they published *Du système pénitentiaire aux Etats-Unis et de son application en France* (1833). Over the next two years Tocqueville wrote his most famous work *De la démocratie en Amérique*, which was published in two parts, in 1835 and 1840. Tocqueville was elected to the Chamber of Deputies in 1839, a position he held until 1848. After the 1848 Revolution he was elected to the Constituent Assembly and for a few months in 1849 he was the foreign minister. Retiring from public life at the end of 1851, Tocqueville occupied his

---

[35] Ibid., 'Another Time'.

[36] For a general account of Tocqueville's life see A. Jardin, *Tocqueville—A Biography*.

[37] J. P. Mayer, *Prophet of the Mass Age*, p. 1. There exists considerable debate as to whether he ever recovered his faith, lost in adolescence. There is, however, little doubt as to the importance that he placed on religion as a social regulator.

last years with the writing of *L'Ancien Régime et la Révolution* (1856). He died on 16 April 1859 in Cannes, and his *Souvenirs* were published posthumously in 1893. Clark's thesis in response to this life is structured along classic lines. Chapter one outlines the work of Tocqueville, while chapters two and three discuss the attraction of the ideal and the conditions that Tocqueville placed on its achievement. The fourth chapter tests the ideal and asks 'is it worth pursuing'? The conclusion draws together the strands of description and critique as Clark reflects on the limits of the liberal creed. But beyond this common formula there are many interesting aspects of the thesis and the historical method that became the hallmark of Clark's later work.

Speaking to a group of graduate students in 1967, and perhaps reflecting on his graduate days, Clark suggested to his audience the provisions that they would need to pack on their journey'.[38] As well as works of John La Nauze and Peter Ryan, the *Shorter Oxford English Dictionary* and 'perhaps a magnifying glass', he suggested that they 'may find it helpful to have another language, and to study economics, statistics, psychology as aids to your work, and for practice in that precision which historians so often lack, to their great damage'.[39] Above all, he hoped that they were 'all believers' in the writing of history. He reminded those who were to analyse society that they belonged to 'a great tradition which includes de Tocqueville and Marx'.[40]

While the thesis is highly critical of Tocqueville and the liberalism he advocated, Clark never devalues the 'great tradition' that Tocqueville represented. This is made all the more evident by the method Clark adopts. As with many of Clark's narrators, the thought can never be divorced from the thinker. Thus James Cook, William Charles Wentworth, Henry Lawson, Robert Menzies and John Curtin are human beings first, and advocates of an ideal second. So to under-

---

[38] M. Clark, *Speaking Out of Turn*, p. 77.
[39] Ibid., p. 78.
[40] Ibid.

stand Tocqueville we must first look at the 'Man and [the] Ideal'.

Tocqueville, we learn, is by birth and temperament an aristocrat. Yet by intellect he was aware his caste's way of life was doomed by democracy's edicts. This became Tocqueville's conundrum, and the central framework of his work: the need to 'reconcile the sentiments of a lively heart with the conclusions of an active mind'.[41] Tocqueville is portrayed as a man out of step with his world, a man brought to tears with the execution of one of his own (Louis XVI) yet bored and contemptuous of the lifestyle of his class. Equally, he is dismayed by the material claims of the working class. Even their manner and approach to life filled him with 'shock and disgust'.[42] The French radical Blanqui, for instance, was judged unworthy because he 'wore a dirty collar'.[43] The believer in democracy and student of America was unable to accept that in the United States 'everyone shook hands irrespective of class or creed'.[44]

In 1962, when Clark wrote of an afternoon 'at the footy', he chided those who would reflect on the 'low-brow' nature of the event or provide sinister explanations for its crowds.[45] It is this inability to stomach working-class culture, or indeed an event that could fill the Members' as well as the Outer, that Clark found so inexplicable in Tocqueville. Tocqueville, like 'the philistines want[s] to take this pleasure away from the people'.[46] Ultimately, it is Tocqueville's callous disregard for the welfare of the poor and the weak that draws Clark's sternest criticism. The story of a working-class girl who expresses the revolutionary opinion that one day her kind would 'be the ones eating the chickens' wings' fills Tocqueville with 'disgust'.[47] The fact that he was so offended by the

---

[41] See p. 58.
[42] See p. 112.
[43] See p. 113.
[44] See p. 72.
[45] Manning Clark, 'At the Footy' published as 'Dons and Blues' in *Nation*, 6 October 1962, reprinted in *Occasional Writings and Speeches*, p. 157.
[46] Ibid., p. 159.
[47] See p. 113.

behaviour of those who would propose to build 'heaven on earth',[48] condemning them as 'rabid materialists',[49] does not escape Clark's criticism. Central to Tocqueville's ideal is the role of religion. If liberty is to do what is 'good and just without compulsion',[50] then what is 'good and just' was supplied by religious belief. Clark responds to this argument with a reflection on both Tocqueville and on the ideal. Tocqueville, Clark noted, wanted to be a believer, yet could not be. As a student, we are told, he studied religion and philosophy to provide him with 'a guide to conduct, a reassurance, not the damping conclusion that man was never sure of anything'.[51] Yet he was reluctant to assent to the doctrines of religion. What is presented in Tocqueville is a struggle between his heart and mind. Clark portrayed this struggle between 'Sodom' and the 'Madonna' as a choice between 'honest materialism' and the will of God.[52] The theme of Sodom and the Madonna was to be used throughout Clark's writings to depict a struggle between doubt and belief.[53] For instance, Marcus Clarke's loss of faith is depicted as a reluctant conversion to a theory of materialism.[54] As Clarke writes:

> Happy is the man who can believe! I cannot. But I am no desperate destroyer; no denier of God and Heaven! I am rather, as one who, wandering through the pleasant gardens of Faith and implicit belief, has stumbled upon the stern rocks that border them; the rocks of Reason and Practicality and Materialism, and stunned by the fall is no more able to return to the pleasant paths and rest with heart at ease upon the dewy turf . . .[55]

God is deployed in Tocqueville's argument in two ways. First, God is a justification. To fail to do what is 'good and

---

[48] See pp. 141–2.
[49] See p. 112.
[50] See p. 54.
[51] See p. 68.
[52] See p. 69.
[53] See G. P. Shaw, 'A Sentimental Humanist', p. 37, and J. Rickard, 'Clark and Patrick White', p. 50.
[54] C. M. H. Clark, *A History of Australia*, vol. IV, pp. 231–2.
[55] Quoted in ibid., p. 231.

just' is to resist the will of God.[56] In the second instance, God's will is a matter of social control. Religion is the 'big stick' wielded to subdue the passions of the bourgeoisie and the working class alike.[57] It is used as a means to direct humankind (and especially the working class) away from base material advancement to higher things.

Clark is quick to highlight the flaws in Tocqueville's use of God as both justification and control. Firstly, Clark notes that for the workers in France, faced with poverty and deprivation, the 'vision of a blessed relief faded from their minds'.[58] Their faith diminished. As Clark was later to comment: 'God is dead—either men shall be as gods, or become citizens of the kingdom of nothingness'.[59] This theme of the loss of faith and the descent into the 'kingdom of nothingness' was to recur throughout Clark's work.[60] Yet it is here in the thesis that Clark first deals with the consequences for a world in which the people have killed their gods.

The second criticism that Clark makes of Tocqueville's use of religion is its divisive nature. The preferred belief, like what is 'good', provides no universal standard. The standards that Tocqueville extols are those in the interests of his own class. Religion becomes a sham if it stands in the way of material progress of the poor at the pleasure of the wealthy. Moreover, the deterrent that Tocqueville provides is no deterrent at all. If religious belief is the deterrent (in the absence of compulsion) then, according to Clark, individuals are at the mercy of the Bonapartists, in Tocqueville's time, and 'in ours the Fascists'.[61]

Clark tests the fundamental aspect of Tocqueville's argument: that is, liberty is to do what is 'good and just without compulsion'.[62] Clark has no doubt that liberty is essential to

---

[56] See p. 76.
[57] See pp. 69–70.
[58] See p. 119.
[59] M. Clark, *Speaking Out of Turn*, p. 118.
[60] See, for example, C. M. H. Clark, *A History of Australia*, vol. IV, chapter 12.
[61] See p. 143.
[62] See p. 54.

society, but can that liberty be secured without compulsion? This basic premise, that individuals should be free from compulsion, has been a strong tenet in liberal philosophy. For instance, Isaiah Berlin in his classic work, 'Two Concepts of Liberty', draws a distinction between 'negative' and 'positive' liberty. The former conception of liberty endorses the view that an individual is negatively free to the 'degree to which no man or body of men interferes with my activity'.[63] The locus of freedom for the individual is determined by the maximisation of non-interference: 'The wider the area of non-interference the wider my freedom'.[64]

Berlin defines 'positive' liberty as 'the wish on the part of the individual to be his own master'.[65] That is, liberty requires more than just the absence of interference—it requires that the individual takes some active steps to gain self-mastery. Berlin's condemnation of 'positive' liberty is based on the paradox that the end result of such self-mastery is the imposition of one's will on another. For Berlin, and the liberalism that he represents, institutions such as the law do interfere with individuals and as such restrict liberty. He says that 'Law is always a "fetter", even if it protects you from being bound in chains that are heavier than those of the law, say, some more repressive law or custom, or arbitrary despotism or chaos'.[66]

Tocqueville shared a similar view of liberty. To modify an individual's aspirations or desires by compulsion was to limit their liberty. Tocqueville's answer to social inequity was a change of heart: 'For then the rich would *voluntarily* share their wealth with the poor'.[67] Clark tests this 'assumption as to compulsion' in chapter four, and finds Tocqueville wanting. In the *Souvenirs*, Tocqueville's response to the June rising is, according to Clark, at odds with his basic ideal: 'The ideal is

---

[63] I. Berlin, 'Two Concepts of Liberty' in *Four Essays on Liberty*, p. 122.
[64] Ibid., p. 123.
[65] Ibid., p. 131.
[66] Ibid., p. 123.
[67] See p. 103.

put aside in the crisis. In a test case he finds order to be a greater good than liberty'.[68]

Clark's condemnation of liberalism must be seen as a response to the perceived inability of Tocqueville's ideal to provide for the material progress of the poor, and the troubling consequences of Europe falling under a Fascist dictatorship. With views that jar our modern sensibilities—yet reflect the stark realities of his time—Clark states that: 'What I have tried to stress is the consequences of excluding compulsion. It excludes action against two great problems in our society: poverty and the use of the liberties to establish a Fascist dictatorship'.[69] Clark continues:

> The fatal helplessness of the liberal ideal must be avoided. It should not be beyond the power of man to devise deterrents and prohibitions which would effectively suppress the 'toughs' without shocking the sensibilities of the men of good will.[70]

It is at this point that Clark parts company with the debilitating consequences of Tocqueville's ideal.

Clark reflects on the historical enterprise—in particular, his own search for a story to tell and the means by which to tell it. The work is indeed one of the first offerings of the apprentice historian.[71] The opening words of chapter one offer a striking and constant theme in Clark's work: 'Historians and dramatists have always had one thing in common. Both have sought to entertain or instruct'.[72] Nearly half a century later Clark remained true to this pronouncement. Speaking in 1984 he told his audience that 'Historians should be judged by their success in increasing wisdom and understanding, and their capacity to entertain'.[73] Clearly, Clark entertained his audiences, but did he retreat from his claim to instruct? In

---

[68] See p. 114.
[69] See p. 143.
[70] Ibid., p. 145.
[71] See M. Clark, *A Historian's Apprenticeship*, and R. M. Crawford, M. Clark and G. Blainey, *Making History*.
[72] See p. 48.
[73] M. Clark, *Speaking Out of Turn*, p. 133.

the epilogue to Volume VI of the *History* the mood has changed somewhat. The historian, like the poet and priest, had ceased to 'draw the maps'. Australians lived in an age when historians could tell the story of how the world came to be, but beyond that they could merely present choices. The change in Clark's tone is subtle, yet it represents both an appreciation of the vicissitudes of life and the fact that the stark choices of October 1938 had receded.

Clark in the thesis is sceptical of the historical method which involved the selective citation of prestigious authors, such as Tocqueville, to bolster a weak argument.[74] For instance, he is critical of barren questions such as: was Tocqueville a Marxist? Or was he a Royalist? Such questions, he felt, told more about the author than the subject. However, Clark was fulsome in his praise of Tocqueville's objectives and methods. He had an 'inquiring eye'. He wanted to know 'the causes of events, the sources of human action, the motives which have governed the actions of both himself and his neighbours'.[75] Clark states: 'We may well judge the talents of a historian by the questions he asks, and Tocqueville not only asks the right questions, but provides answers which have stood the test of time'.[76] When Clark returned later to the theme of the role and method of historians, many of the features he associated with and admired in Tocqueville were repeated.

Manning Clark's 'debt to Alexis de Tocqueville was obvious and profound'.[77] Indeed, the French historian became a crucial stimulus for a lifelong pursuit that not only saw Clark ponder the great questions of humankind, but also set him upon a path that resulted in his classic six-volume *History of Australia*. He records the genesis of his research on Tocqueville as taking place in Humphrey Sumner's study at Oxford in 1938. It was Sumner who suggested that Clark write an essay

---

[74] See p. 48.
[75] See p. 70.
[76] See p. 129.
[77] G. P. Shaw, 'A Sentimental Humanist', p. 38.

on *Souvenirs,* and he went on to uncover the motives behind his supervisory nudge:

> Tocqueville, he said, is your man: he is interested in what you are interested in—the effect of a mass age on a culture, the question whether equality and liberty are compatible with each other. And, he added, there was more to it than that: 'Tocqueville, like you Clark, wanted to believe.' But before I could even say a yes, let alone ask how he knew so much about me in such a little time, I was made aware that I was not to ask questions about what went on in his mind. From that day we understood each other, but I never dared to make a personal remark to him.[78]

Despite the importance of Tocqueville to Clark's intellectual development, he receives only a handful of express references in the *History.* This is not to underplay the powerful rhetorical and conceptual framework that Tocqueville provided. Indeed, in Volume IV, 'The Earth Abideth For Ever', Clark describes the emotional division of Charles Cowper, whose values encompassed those of the 'country squire' with its loathing of popular government, and a realisation, like that of Tocqueville, that the victory of democracy is inevitable.[79] For further reference to these arguments Clark advises readers to 'see vols 2 and 3 of this history'.[80] While this open referencing may have frustrated his critics, in Tocqueville's case it was obviously true. In fact, Clark could easily have advised readers to 'see vols 1 to 6', such was the backdrop that Tocqueville played for the *History.*

Clark marshalled Tocqueville throughout his writing in two ways. The first relates to Tocqueville as the standard-bearer for the dilemma of the Enlightenment. In this form Tocqueville admonishes one, and provides succour for another, of the three great faiths that Clark deployed to tell his story of Australia. Just as Catholicism, Protestantism and

---

[78] Ibid., p. 63.
[79] C. M. H. Clark, *A History of Australia,* vol. IV, p. 36.
[80] Ibid.

the Enlightenment provided a tripod upon which Clark could survey Australia, Tocqueville's contribution was as a reliable critic for the Enlightenment's vision splendid and as a support for the Protestant ascendancy. It is to Tocqueville that Clark turns when he is providing the intellectual grounding for Australia's conservatives. As with William Charles Wentworth, Richard Baker and Robert Menzies, the lesson of Tocqueville was the danger of the unfettered will of the people. For these, and the other inhabitants of 'Yarraside', the challenge of the Enlightenment was to overturn superstition. The craving for 'uncommonly large profits' was to be thwarted with the tools that Tocqueville, John Stuart Mill, Edmund Burke and others had provided. For these architects of colonial administration, of the Commonwealth Constitution and of post-World War II Australia, the answer was to create institutions to provide political equality at the same time as 'ensuring the survival of the institutions of private industry and the profit incentive'.[81]

But in Clark's work, Tocqueville is more than an apologist for the comfortable classes. In his second form Tocqueville provides a voice for many of the concerns that Clark himself shared. The need for many 'voices' in a narrative history is obvious, though for Clark there are two particular 'voices' that need to be harmonised. They are the faith of Henry Lawson and Victor Daley, which hoped to 'steal fire from heaven', and the darker voice that kept reminding Clark of the great folly of the human heart. As he stated, it is

> ... the task of the storyteller to create a harmony between those two voices—the one which believes that we can steal fire from heaven, and the one which believes that no human events are worth taking seriously, that there is madness in our hearts while we live, and after that we go to the dead.[82]

It was Tocqueville who helped introduce Clark to the 'madness in our hearts' and who caused him to question the hopes and aspirations of the Enlightenment:

---

[81] C. M. H. Clark, *A History of Australia*, vol. V, p. 66.
[82] Clark, *A Discovery of Australia*, p. 55.

As a young man I had written a thesis on Alexis de Tocqueville. He fashioned my thinking about the world in which I lived. He put into words the great question raised by the American and French revolutions: Can there be equality without restraints on liberty, without mediocrity, without conformism and without spiritual bullying? Will the majority in a democracy tyrannise over the minority?[83]

Like Tocqueville, Clark questions the vision which the Enlightenment offered and particularly the capacity of humankind to rise to its challenges. As he acknowledges:

More examples of human behaviour strengthened my conviction that the heart did not contain that jewel of perfection in which the gurus of the Enlightenment wanted me to believe. Perhaps I had what de Tocqueville labelled 'un goût dépravé' for examples of human madness. I was a drunkard for the dark side of the human heart.[84]

These two themes, of liberty without tyranny and an obsession with the 'dark side of the human heart', resonate throughout Clark's writing. The first of these represents an aspect of Clark's estrangement from his origins and aspirations. Just as Clark 'stood always a pace or two apart' from his Melbourne heritage and the readers of the Left Book Club and Historical Enterprises Proprietary Limited,[85] so too his lack of faith prevented him from committing himself fully to many of the tenets of the Enlightenment which he so admired. In his 1962 article entitled 'Faith', Clark establishes a dichotomy that unpacks many of the issues that troubled him about the two schools of 'unbelievers'.[86] The dichotomy was based on the familiar Melbourne/Sydney divide. Both represent secular humanism, but both are equally divided over the 'conception of man and the meaning of his life'.[87]

---

[83] Ibid., pp. 57–8.
[84] Clark, *A Historian's Apprenticeship*, p. 5.
[85] S. Macintyre, 'Always a pace or two apart', p. 17.
[86] 'Faith', in P. Coleman (ed.), *Australian Civilization*, 1962 (reprinted in *Occasional Writings and Speeches*, p. 152).
[87] Ibid.

According to Clark, Melbourne represents the bastion of liberalism, secularism, Marxism and the Enlightenment. It is Melbourne which believes in the 'uplifting and spiritual role of culture in the civilisation of the masses' and 'brotherly love'. Sydney, by contrast, is crass and worships beauty over compassion. It ridicules the progressives and meliorism. It is perhaps appropriate that Clark wrote this in Canberra where he maintained his critical distance from both groups of 'unbelievers'.

The second quality that Clark shared with Tocqueville was his fascination with the 'dark side of the human heart'. This prompted Clark to investigate, for instance, the folly and madness of Robert O'Hara Burke. As we read in volume IV of the *History*: 'Nature had planted in him that fatal capacity to be swayed by some malevolent spirit like the Greek goddess Ate, who prompted men to acts of aberration and folly, made them subject to those attacks of the "sillies", which drove them to make wild decisions'.[88] One of the hallmarks of Clark's writings is the presence of the omnipotent narrator who pauses to reflect upon the characters as they take part in the nation's story. His characters are men and women of great passion and despair. More often than not they are afflicted by 'flaws in their clay'. Alfred Deakin and Henry Lawson, the two great narrators of volume V, were afflicted with tormented souls. For Mr Deakin, 'words could not do justice . . . to the tragic grandeur of what had happened to the most distinguished son of the Australian-Britons'.[89] Henry Lawson ended his days a 'wreck'.[90] The *History*, especially after volume III, often reflects upon the dark side of humanity. Individuals strike out with immense folly or crave spoils that remain just outside their reach. As Miriam Dixson puts it: 'War rages in the hearts of Clark's characters, and evil often appears to have the upper hand'.[91]

---

[88] C. M. H. Clark, *A History of Australia*, vol. IV, p. 147.
[89] C. M. H. Clark, *A History of Australia*, vol. V, p. 427.
[90] Ibid.
[91] M. Dixson, 'Clark and National Identity', p. 204.

# In Search of Manning Clark

W HO WAS MANNING CLARK? We have glimpses of him through some of the favoured figures of his *History* and his miscellaneous writings and speeches. Is he Henry Lawson, the city bushman and apostle of mateship, who in forging his view of Australia attempted to banish the 'old-world errors and wrongs and lies'?[92] Is he Fyodor Dostoevsky, epileptic and perennial searcher for the truth of life's mysteries in a world without God? Is he an Old Testament seer or Marxist prophet, speaking out for a generation, willing to comment on and contribute to the shape of the future? Is he Alexis de Tocqueville, historian, attentive student of the human predicament, though a man beset by fears and doubts? Or do we see in Clark elements of each of these men—the passion, aspiration and wisdom, alongside the flaws and failings?

Responses, some trenchant, some simply wrong, to each and all of these possibilities are scattered throughout recent works on Clark such as the Carl Bridge-edited *Manning Clark —Essays on his Place in History* (1994), Stephen Holt's *A Short History of Manning Clark* (1999) and the outpouring of print that followed Peter Ryan's unsavoury attack on Clark in *Quadrant* in 1993 and the Lenin medal farce of 1996.[93] It is not the intention of the editors here to work through this literature. Such an exercise would be neither helpful nor relevant. Rather, do Tocqueville and 'The Ideal of Alexis de Tocqueville' assist us in understanding Manning Clark—the man behind the contentious public profile?

To answer this question, we might start with a revealing passage in Clark's second autobiographical volume *The Quest for Grace* (1990).[94] Published the year before he died, *Quest* recalls the first stages of Clark's personal struggle to understand humanity in an age witnessing a continuing decline of

---

[92] Henry Lawson, 'A Song of the Republic', *Complete Works 1885–1900*, p. 39.

[93] Carl Bridge, ed., *Manning Clark: Essays on his Place in History*; Stephen Holt, *A Short History of Manning Clark*; Peter Ryan, 'Manning Clark', *Quadrant* (1993); Humphrey McQueen, *Suspect History*.

[94] Manning Clark, *The Quest for Grace*.

belief in the teachings of religion. Conscious of early influ-
ences, Clark contrasts two familiar figures, Tocqueville and
Dostoevsky:

> Tocqueville was not a ferocious man. Unlike Dostoevsky,
> Tocqueville did not suffer from the 'falling sickness'. Tocque-
> ville had never spat at a man because he disagreed with his
> ideas, as Dostoevsky spat at Bakunin in Geneva. Tocqueville
> was not a 'great sinner': Tocqueville's past did not drive him, as
> Dostoevsky was driven all his life, to 'redeem the days' of
> which his madness and his folly had robbed him. Unlike Dos-
> toevsky, Tocqueville made no extravagant prophecies, no pre-
> diction that without Christ men would kill each other down to
> the last two men on earth. He made no wild remarks. But he
> knew the dilemma of his day. Religious belief was the essential
> condition of goodness and liberty. But, alas, he himself did not
> and could not believe; he had lost his faith.[95]

While rejecting Tocqueville's class snobbery—his response to
the French radical Blanqui's dirty collar, mentioned in the
thesis, is remembered in *Quest*—Clark acknowledges the
appeal of Tocqueville's demeanour, his scholarly reserve and
intellectual courage. Above all, he empathises with Tocqueville's struggle to reconcile goodness and evil: 'His heart . . .
was a battlefield between the ideal of the Madonna and the
pursuit of Sodom. Working on Tocqueville became part of
the quest for understanding'.[96] A most significant part. The
Tocqueville thesis introduces the reader to the basic foundations of Clark's social and moral stance.

Most of the key elements of the mature Clark are present,
in microcosm, in the 1943 work: an abiding interest in centre-
stage individuals, the big characters as the stuff of history;
the intention to 'tell a story from the past to communicate a
vision of life';[97] the integration of sources, especially literary
sources, to assist the process of understanding, both for writer
and reader; evidence of the historian writing with 'an eye of

---

[95] Ibid., p. 86.
[96] Ibid., p. 87.
[97] Clark, *Speaking Out of Turn*, p. 68.

pity', particularly as this relates to the downtrodden and poor, those people absent from life's great banquet; evidence, too, of the historian casting a critical eye over the manipulators and abusers of the people, or those who would simply ignore their plight; recognition of the madness in the human heart and its expression, often, in the majority's tyrannical sway over the minority; and recognition that, with the decline in religious belief, humanity needed to discover alternative spiritual strategies or face the prospect of desolation—life in the 'Kingdom of Nothingness'. With increasing fervour in the last twenty-five years of his life, Clark sought to encourage his readers and listeners to be believers in human possibility. He wanted them to imagine and contribute to nothing less than a better world.

When Dymphna and Sebastian Clark collected Manning's unpublished speeches and lectures delivered between 1940 and 1991 for the posthumous *Speaking Out of Turn* (1997), they used Manning's cheery Preface, one of the last pieces he wrote.[98] He concludes this Preface by saying that the speeches comprise 'one man's contribution to the ever-increasing band of life-affirmers in Australia: to those who share my hope and my faith that Australia will not always be in the hands of the tough, that it could and should belong to the lovers and believers'.[99] This last phrase had become something of a signature utterance in his twilight years.

No such optimism exists anywhere in the Tocqueville thesis—it is, after all, the product of a young academic comparing and contrasting two chaotic periods of Western history one hundred years apart, and it is written during a global war —but knowledgeable Clark readers will readily discern the way in which the humanist position articulated in this first scholarly work blossomed in later years. Through an appreciation of this continuity, we get closer to the man himself.

'The Ideal of Alexis de Tocqueville' showcases for the first time the kind of historian Manning Clark was destined to

---

[98] Ibid., pp. xvii–xviii.
[99] Ibid., p. xviii.

become. He shapes the complexities of a critical period in post-revolutionary French history for us through a small number of important historical figures, and conveys the subtleties of the time through a detailed study of one seminal individual. Alexis de Tocqueville, politician, writer and commentator on the human condition, could not have been scriptwritten any better to suit Clark's purposes. When choosing the principal figures for the *History*, Clark favoured individuals who like Tocqueville both influenced and transcended their times—and who are able to increase our understanding of the past. Henry Lawson, for example, bears enormous narrative weight in Volume V, 'The People Make Laws' (1899–1915), not only as a superb chronicler of the manners of his community but also because of his contribution to Australian myths of progress and mateship, the city vs the bush, and to Australian nationalism.

Reflecting on his method in *Making History* (1985), Clark conceded the possible limitations of his approach:

> I'm . . . very sorry that I never found the answer to the relationship between the characters in the front of the stage and the backdrop. I was weak on backdrop, I'm still weak on backdrop, but I probably spent too much time on the characters.[1]

While this might be true, it is a method suited to a historian committed to conveying 'a vision of life'. A talk Clark gave on Cardinal Newman, in August 1990, clarifies the connection between the two:

> I felt that if you want to write a history, it must be about some vision of life that you have: some view about human nature, about the complex fate of being a human being, about the great aspirations of humanity.[2]

The big picture needed big characters commensurate with its scale. Clark's study of Tocqueville's ideal provided an essential training ground for the future.

---

[1] Crawford et al., *Making History*, p. 65.
[2] Clark, *Speaking Out of Turn*, p. 203.

The thesis also makes effective use of external sources, not to validate the argument—Clark rejected this technique in any writer—but rather to amplify it. A breadth of French literary and philosophical reference expands the narrative, including Chateaubriand, Montesquieu, Balzac, Vigny, Hugo, Flaubert and Sand. Heinrich Heine and Max Weber are also used. Two other writers appearing in the thesis, Karl Marx and Fyodor Dostoevsky, were destined to play more important roles in the Clark *oeuvre*. He would ultimately refer to them, along with Moses, Isaiah, Job, Christ, Tolstoy, Newman and Lenin, as among 'the great teachers of mankind'.[3] Throughout his life, Clark enthusiastically conveyed the views of those writers he felt had something to say that mattered.

The most important prefiguring of Clark's *History* provided by the Tocqueville thesis relates to the range of binaries implicit within it: intelligentsia/working classes, aristocracy/ working classes, fascism/Marxism, civilised/uncivilised and refinement/coarseness. Clark barely contains his disdain for Tocqueville's aloof circle of 'refined intellectuals' and the Frenchman's belief that 'personal taste' was more important than having a strong opinion on an issue. Nor can he disguise his sympathy for 'the rough and tumble life of the masses' that Tocqueville rejected. Tocqueville, the thesis maintains in so many words, was a man far more comfortable in the Melbourne Clubs of his day, rather than the MCG.

Clark's most serious criticism of Tocqueville, however, stems directly from the Frenchman's class-based views: namely, his inability to dirty his hands in what he perceived as the trough of social improvement. Clark extends a far better metaphor in chapter IV, 'The Test':

> . . . if fraternity is a stimulant for reconciliation Tocqueville must have drunk a very sour brand. Not only were his teeth on edge; his mind too was antagonistic to these men who dreamed of a new heaven on earth.[4]

---

[3] Ibid., p. 177.
[4] See p. 119.

Here is the conclusion to Clark's case, that Tocqueville recognised much that was wrong, conceived of a good society, yet finally would do nothing to bring about its realisation. At the end of chapter IV, Clark's argument leaves the reader with a clear choice:

> Marx exhorted his contemporaries to speed up the advent of the new society—action would bring the day near. Tocqueville counsels resignation and renunciation of this world. Redemption will come not in this world but in the next.[5]

Clark was not prepared to accept the argument or the wait.

The six-volume *History* abounds with stark choices—between 'the old dead tree' (the British in Australia) and 'the young tree green' (cultivation of an Australian sentiment);[6] between those who embrace the Kingdom of Nothingness and those who would have life and have it more abundantly; between the straiteners and the enlargers, life deniers and life affirmers, discouragers and encouragers; and between those Australians committed to a bright future for their country and those he would label the 'addicts of Englishmanism', utilising a term that Daniel Henry Deniehy used in 1854 to describe the cringing behaviour of Henry Parkes.[7]

At the end of the chapter in *The Quest for Grace* entitled 'Mr Passion on the Shores of Corio Bay', Manning Clark reviews the many contending voices inside him as he left Geelong Grammar School on 1 May 1944 to take up a lectureship at the University of Melbourne. The last of these is that of 'a young man who had already decided the measurers, the social scientists and the spiritual bullies were disastrously wrong, but who did not know what was right, or what he had to offer'.[8] On reaching the epilogue to the final volume of the *History*, over forty years and many books, lectures and speeches later, he had a finely developed sense of what was

---

[5] See p. 131.
[6] See Clark, *Speaking Out of Turn*, p. 141.
[7] Manning Clark, *In Search of Henry Lawson*, p. 26.
[8] Clark, *The Quest for Grace*, p. 145.

right and wrong, and what he had offered. He pondered the fate of a nation where 'the people broke the Tablets of the Law. The people killed their gods. The people turned to worship of the Golden Calf'.[9] In the end, all that appeared to remain of the three great European faiths brought to Australia was the craving for 'uncommonly large profit'. But Clark did not despair. He answered Tocqueville's 'what then?' It was the task of a new generation to be wiser than the previous one, to aspire to be lovers and believers:

> They can make their own history. With the end of the domination by the straiteners, the enlargers of life now have their chance. They have the chance to lavish on each other the love the previous generations had given to God, and to bestow on the here and now the hope and dreams they had once entertained for some future human harmony.[10]

It may be that for Clark, a child of the Enlightenment in life-long rebellion, faith and hope, rather than self-interest, are all that can be believed in: 'Within the darkness in the human heart there was beauty. Inside the darkness there was grace'.[11]

---

[9] C. M. H. Clark, *A History of Australia*, vol. VI, p. 500.

[10] Ibid.

[11] Clark, *A Discovery of Australia*, p. 62.

# THE IDEAL

## OF

# ALEXIS DE TOCQUEVILLE

## BY

# C. M. H. CLARK

# Contents

# PREFACE

October 1938 was an unpropitious moment to begin historical research: the lights of the 'low, dishonest decade' were flickering fitfully; only the Cliveden set and the pacifists were striving to keep them alight. Some students comforted themselves with the reflection that Boethius had written his *Consolation of Philosophy* as the barbarians were sacking Rome, while Henri Pirenne had written his *History of Europe* without books or notes, as a Belgian prisoner of war in Germany. In retrospect the hopes with which we calmed our troubled minds seem not only pretentious but pathetic. We clung desperately to the illusion that our activities were important, though no one knew why. Even on Friday September 1st, 1939, none of the regular readers at the Bodleian were absent. At lunch time the attendant merely asked us to bring our gas masks in the afternoon. Research as usual appeared to be the motto of the students. If the past was our escape from the present, at least there was a tacit assumption that this painful reproach should not be mentioned in our presence. And what better introduction to dreamland could the student have than the musty tomes and the sheltered rooms of the Bodleian Library?

In the interval between the Munich Agreement and German invasion of Poland, my supervisor at Balliol College, Mr B. H. Sumner, suggested that I should write my thesis on Alexis de Tocqueville. The idea appealed to me. Was not Tocqueville the best representative of that liberal creed which had promised the good society to its followers and left them with poverty, anarchy and war? A study of Tocqueville would perhaps help to explain why this had occurred. After reading his works I felt strongly that one reason for this tragic legacy of the liberal creed was the gulf between their ideal and their behaviour. They believed that all men should be able to live 'the good life', by which they understood the life of the polite intellectuals of their day. They were deluded on two points: it was not easy to persuade the mass of mankind that their way of life was the best—(Tocqueville perceived this, but refused to modify his ideal); secondly, they were simply not prepared to accept the political and social changes necessary if all were to pursue their good life.

At least that was my impression after the first reading of the published works of Tocqueville. Work on the unpublished manuscripts at Tocqueville, especially the correspondence, strengthened this judgement. Unfortunately the outbreak of war abruptly ended my work on this material. Since then I have read the contemporaries of Tocqueville, and discerned the same illusions in their works. After one year spent collecting material and four years of teaching, I had neither the time nor the material for a definitive work on the man, while the vivid impressions of that first exciting year have been blurred. The work as it stands does not pretend to be more than an interpretation of Tocqueville to prove the ideas which rushed into my mind when I first read his work.

I should like to thank Professor Crawford of the University of Melbourne and Mr B. H. Sumner of Balliol College for both advice and inspiration; also the present Comte de Tocqueville, for permission to examine the unpublished material preserved in the Château at Tocqueville. My wife quickened my interest in things European, restrained my wayward impulses as an interpreter and translator, and, in general, made certain that the idea of writing something on the 'Toccers' (as we called the notes) did not remain an idle day-dream.

For the convenience of those who are not familiar with the life of Tocqueville, the main events are tabulated in Appendix I. A full list of the material consulted is given in the bibliographical note. The references are placed at the end of the text [here, at the end of each chapter—eds].

C M H Clark
University of Melbourne

# CHAPTER I
## Introduction

Historians and dramatists have always had one thing in common. Both have sought to entertain or to instruct. Their instruction was effective as long as the audience was not sceptical of the sanction for their opinions. But God disappeared from the pages of history books just as His appearances on the stage became less and less frequent. Instruction without the aid of divine sanction placed a severe strain on the skill of the writer. Readers no longer approached the historical treatise in reverent mood. Some hoped for a pleasant distraction; others required serious enlightenment, on the strict condition that the author flattered their prejudices, or at least respected their sensibilities. Yet despite the loss of their trump card, dramatists and historians have persuaded their audiences to accept their opinions. How? By substituting human prestige for the divine recommendation. To justify resignation, some quote Macbeth's soliloquy; to silence the opponents of social reform others recite an epigram by Shaw. The success or failure of a polemic often depends on the writer's skill in quoting authors who enjoy a prestige with the readers he is seeking to influence. The subject of this work is a man who enjoys this prestige with those who believe in the values of the liberals—Alexis-Charles-Henri Clérel de Tocqueville.[a]

---

[a] On p. 4 of the copy text of his thesis, Clark inserts a marginal note: 'Revise—retain idea—but remove "clumsy" expression'. These revisions were made (in manuscript) and have been incorporated in this edition.

Before we comment on the use made of Tocqueville's prestige, it is necessary to notice how it was acquired. It begins with a power to elicit sympathy with what he is trying to do. In his lifetime the only unsympathetic review of his work came from the pen of a man whose affection for the *Ancien Régime* was so strong that any writer not sharing his desire to restore it was *ipso facto* damned.[1] But except for this one dissenting voice, men as remote from one another as Peel and John Stuart Mill, writers as different as Heine and Lamennais, politicians from the Right and the Left such as Guizot and Louis Blanc referred sympathetically to his work. Even those who attempted to ridicule him were either politicians like Thiers, who lacked the very quality which Tocqueville was recommending—enthusiasm for the good society[2]—or dramatists like Pailleron, who believed that it was the function of Gallic humour to administer cold douches to the serious-minded.[3]

Even in his lifetime, politicians used his prestige to support the opinions they were advocating at the hustings or at Westminster and Paris. The habit of quoting Tocqueville was so common in the French Chamber of Deputies that Thiers was able to ridicule his opponents by adding ironically the phrase '. . . *comme disait M. de Tocqueville* . . .' [as Monsieur de Tocqueville said] to every argument he used.[4] His three volumes on American democracy were welcomed not only as a standard work on the subject, but as a prophecy of the development of European social and political institutions—a fact which is illustrated by the number of people who have commented on his powers as a prophet.[5]

Nor are the comments made since his death any less sympathetic or respectful. When Dicey quoted Tocqueville's terse judgement on the English Constitution—'*elle n'existe point*' [it doesn't exist at all]—to prove that the English had no written constitution, he was starting a tradition which has continued till the present. Tocqueville's opinions enjoy a prestige with the class of people interested in the exchange of ideas.

Perhaps we should do well to define the limits of this prestige. It does not, as far as I know, extend beyond this class. The opinions which excite and inspire the intelligentsia rouse little if any response from the masses; the learned pay homage to his influence, but the popular pamphleteer ignores him. Nor are the publishers of cheap editions responsive to the appeals of the learned to make the public more familiar with his opinions.[6] The second limit is that his prestige never renders him an object of reverence; no writer has treated him with that religious awe which silences criticism and makes doubt profane or even blasphemous. Nor did Tocqueville himself claim to possess superhuman powers—an important point for the critic because it relieves him from asking the difficult question: did he possess those powers, and if so, are they a sufficient recommendation for his opinions?

But perhaps it is simpler when authors do claim to possess those powers. At least there is a clear distinction between the believers and the sceptics. Certainly the modern intelligentsia are suspicious of those teachers who claim to possess superhuman powers, but they are apparently disposed to accept the opinions of those who have acquired prestige. Writers on contemporary problems tend to ignore or to sneer at the reverence formerly paid to religious teachers, while they themselves sprinkle their books liberally with quotations from the writings of the men with prestige. The assumption is that the validity of their opinions becomes greater in proportion to the number of authors they can cite as supporters of their position. A good example of this method is Mr Leonard Woolf's work *The Barbarians at the Gate*. Mr Woolf wanted to persuade his readers that his own conception of the good life was the best. To do this he shows that his values have the approval of Pericles, Plato, Christ and Marx—the suggestion being that agreement with Mr Woolf is also evidence of the superior qualities of the reader, superior because he accepts the values of the wisest and best. This type of performance—and there have been many of them—would not be used unless the authors and readers thought that affinity with the great was a very strong recommendation and a very pleasing reassurance. And once it is recognised as persuasive, the task of the authors using the method is to select from a number of writers with prestige the opinions which concur with their own and to present them under a striking title—*Jack Smith, Prophet of Socialism*, or *Jim Roberts and the Question of Free Trade*.

Significantly enough, all the works on Tocqueville published since 1918 belong to this category; their authors are simply using him as a support for their own opinions. Monsieur A. Rédier, a French Catholic with royalist sympathies, wrote his *Comme disait M. de Tocqueville* to persuade his readers that France should abolish the Third Republic, restore the monarchy and introduce a Christian authoritarian régime.[7] In 1932, Professor Laski, an English professor of Political Science with socialist leanings, wrote an essay on Tocqueville to prove that he (Tocqueville) agreed with the main historical conclusions of Marx—'Tocqueville saw hardly less clearly than Marx the disharmony of interests between masters and men in a capitalist democracy. He underlined hardly less emphatically its probable issue in revolution'.[8]

The conscientious reader, fresh from the smooth arguments of M. Rédier, may gasp at this Protean figure who supports both the Vatican and the Kremlin, but a plunge into the more recent literature on the subject will distract his mind from the puzzle of reconciling M. Rédier and Professor Laski. He will be told that Tocqueville's special genius was as a prophet—'the prophet of the mass age'—the predictor of the fascist régimes which have sprung up in Europe in the last decade like mushrooms after heavy rain.[9] The implication in this work is that because he warns Europeans of this phenomenon he has a message for those who wish to preserve 'the eternal principles of the West' (whatever they may be). But, alas, interest in the prophets of fascism is waning: familiarity breeds contempt. Still there is one prophecy by Tocqueville waiting to be used: his belief that the future lay with the Anglo-Saxon and the Slav. Even if this would not have been regarded as a popular news item in August 1939, surely now, in October 1943 it is a stop press message![10]

The objections to this type of interpretation are not the apparent contradictions in the conclusions reached by the various authors. They are intelligible if we remember their political sympathies. Nor are we suggesting that any one of these authors has been guilty of deliberate intellectual dishonesty. There is evidence in Tocqueville's writings to support all their opinions. But when authors limit their discussions to such questions as: was Tocqueville a Marxist, or was he a royalist, or did he prophesy the Nazi party, his opinions tend to recede to the back of the canvas while the opinions of the author, and his authority—Marx, or the Popes, or Max Weber—tend to dominate the foreground. The work becomes a selection of the Marxist or royalist or prophetic pronouncements of Tocqueville. Sometimes Tocqueville performs the function of a magic looking-glass, so that when Professor Laski collects the opinions of Tocqueville on the class struggle and presents them in an attractive form, we may be learning more about Laski than about Tocqueville. We would learn even more about Professor Laski if he stated his position without referring to the teachers of the past.

This does not mean that it is stupid to ask a person: are you a Marxist? We may learn a lot about the person from the answer which he gives. But the reader of Professor Laski's essay may infer that because there is a similarity between Marx and Tocqueville in their analysis of the problems of their age, they would agree in their recommendations. Alas, to accept the fact of the class struggle does not entail a belief in the necessity for socialism. In June of 1848 Marx and Tocqueville were on opposite sides of the barricade. Indeed it may be more useful to inquire why men with similar analyses and similar aims—the good of mankind—fought in different camps in the showdown of 1848. But more of that later.

The opinions of a writer with prestige are persuasive only to those who are disposed to be persuaded. It may be reassuring to the doubters to know that Plato, Hume or Kant is on their side— provided of course that they are impressed by these teachers, or frequent a society where approval of their opinions is warmly received. In providing this reassurance, history is performing a similar function to a metaphysical concept: it is both a comforter and a recommendation for opinions and behaviour. But just as some men were less impressed by the metaphysical consolations of Christianity than by Christian ethics, so we would do well to apply the same distinction to the opinions allegedly supported by Tocqueville. Ignore the prestige and the build-up of a hundred years of eulogy and adulation, and find out first the ideal of this man whom our intelligentsia flatter so profusely by frequent quotation.

There is however a third and, we believe, a stronger reason for being sceptical about the conclusions reached by these authors. All three assume that if we acted on the advice of Tocqueville, as interpreted by his commentators, we would have a <u>better</u> world. The technique is: it is not only I, the author of this book, who am telling you this, but also Tocqueville, a very great man etc.

It is at this point that the critics will pose a very awkward question: do I approve of the world they are recommending to me? Sympathy with an ideal often evaporates when it is translated into language which clarifies the behaviour required to achieve it. Men may experience ecstasy when they are told of the fruits of brotherly love, but the same men may become very angry with its apostles if they insist on the renunciation of worldly goods. They may justify their repudiation of the ideal with the argument that too high a price is required for its achievement. Then the original sympathy with and attraction to the ideal are swamped by repugnance for the actions which it entails. Perhaps some may allow the ideal to float across their mind as a consolation when the results of its repudiation become acutely painful—for example in war-time. But by the strong-minded, even this would be condemned as empty day-dreaming.

At least most men observe the principle that when the price of an ideal is excessively high it is not worth pursuing. It is because I wish to observe the empirical principles, noticing what would in fact occur if Tocqueville's ideal were applied, that I entertain the profoundest doubts concerning it. Whether it is attainable or not I am uncertain, and am content to leave the decision to the reader. But of one thing I am certain: if it were attained the evil results would be greater than the good. For these reasons, I am sceptical of the performance of recent commentators, and suggest a more elementary inquiry: what was Tocqueville's ideal; what methods did he postulate to attain it; and is it worth pursuing?

Men of goodwill may be irritated or angered by the absence of enthusiasm in this discussion of his ideal. Surely it is outrageous, even impious, to be critical of a man whose ideal is liberty. But then approval or disapproval depends not so much on the zeal with which he propagated his faith, but on the quality of the 'liberty'.

After all, even the Nazis are enthusiasts for liberty. And it is as well to be on one's guard when discussing his conception, because at first sight it is a very pleasing one: liberty is to do what is good and just without compulsion.* Everyone pays homage to goodness, while compulsion is felt to be irksome or intolerable. And it is possibly because men feel such warm sympathy with these sentiments that they have strongly approved of the work of Alexis de Tocqueville— an uncritical approval if we may judge by their failure to notice the consequences of accepting his position.

Yet these consequences are abundantly clear from his own elaboration of the ideal. For it is one thing to urge men to pursue the good life, and quite another to ensure that they will pursue it. With Tocqueville this difficulty is intensified by the exacting standards which he set for the good life—the affection for the pleasures of the mind, and for refinement and the renunciation of the pleasures of the common man, that is, of material well-being. Not only was his good life unattractive to all but the very few, but the conditions he laid down for its attainment were very hard: he insisted that the only admissible agent therefore must be the free exercise of the individual's mind. Within the limits defined by God, man was free to choose his own way of life; there must be no compulsion. What is implied is that if men exercise this power of free choice they will decide to pursue the good life. At least this was the theory; experience, as we shall see, made him very sceptical.

Now what Tocqueville saw very clearly was that if men were to pursue this ideal, they must have certain 'liberties': there must be no restrictions imposed either by law or by custom on their power

---

* This definition of liberty is not taken from Tocqueville's own words but from a passage by John Winthrop quoted by Tocqueville in Tome I, p. 67 of *De la Démocratie en Amérique*. His agreement with Winthrop's definition is amply demonstrated in the fulsome praise which he bestowed on it: *'Cette sainte liberté nous devons la défendre dans tous les hasards, et exposer, s'il le faut, pour elle notre vie.'* [We must defend this sainted liberty at all costs, if need be, risking our lives.] (ibid., p. 67). It is, I think, significant that Tocqueville made only two attempts to define his conception of liberty: one in this passage, where he used the words of another man, and the other in *Ancien Régime, OE. C.* IV. p. 248. [See 'Tocqueville and the Translations', Appendix.]

to think, to write, to speak or to associate with their fellow-men. Liberty, by his definition, entailed the 'liberties'—political liberty, liberty of association, liberty of the press. Yet might not these liberties be used, not for what was good and just, but for what was evil and contemptible? Men might use the liberty of the press to persuade others to hold certain opinions or to vote for candidates who intended to abolish these liberties; they might use liberty of association to form political parties whose aims were incompatible with his ideal. So the first problem which Tocqueville attempts to answer is: will men use the liberties to do what is good and just? His answer is: not unless some effective restraint on their behaviour is found. The values of men living in an industrial society—their affection for material well-being, their indifference to the fate of others, disposed their minds to accept <u>any</u> government which could guarantee the conditions for the peaceful pursuit of material prosperity.

Tocqueville believed that religious beliefs provided the restraint upon values and behaviour; that they were an effective antidote to material satisfactions, to indifference and selfishness. More, he believed that a man who accepted the '*discipline supérieure*' [higher discipline] would always use his liberties to do what was good and just. Not that Tocqueville's answer is limited by the conviction: men with religious beliefs will always think and behave in a desirable way. On the contrary, he insisted that the type of society men lived in had an important influence on opinions and behaviour. Indeed, he doubted whether any society where wealth was very unequally distributed would maintain its liberties for long. Because he believed that equality was essential to liberty he came to believe in equality as the social setting for his ideal. In the second and third chapters I intend to discuss the type of person attracted to this ideal and the effectiveness of the conditions prescribed for its pursuit—religious beliefs and equality.

In the fourth chapter I shall attempt to answer the question: is his ideal worth pursuing? The criterion will be not so much Tocqueville's declared intentions, as the practical consequences which attended his efforts to uphold his ideal in the face of events. We shall see that a faithful pursuit of the ideal entails results which are undesirable.

The first and most obvious consequence of accepting his ideal is a repudiation of violence as a means to achieve political or social reform. This antipathy to violence, which does credit to his heart, was difficult to follow in a society which had progressed mainly by its use. A scrupulous observance of this principle also placed its followers at a disadvantage in their competition for power over the minds and hearts of French citizens, against those who were not inhibited by such scruples.

The second consequence is entailed in his definition of the 'good'. When Tocqueville pronounces the spiritual satisfactions to be superior to the material ones, few would disagree with him, and even those who did would probably find, after a prolonged and heated discussion, that the pleasures they value were the same as his. But Tocqueville goes further and condemns all men and parties who insist that material well-being is essential to the pursuit of the good life. This does not mean that he believes men ought to experience poverty to enrich their souls—happily we do not find that argument in his works; on the contrary, he wants to improve the conditions of the working classes. But it does mean that he refers to this principle to justify his opposition to every party which proposed to improve the material well-being of the working classes by practical measures. How long would the working classes have to wait for relief from poverty, if men with the values of Tocqueville were to be their guardians?[b]

Perhaps the most serious objection to his ideal is the uncompromising repudiation of compulsion. For those whose minds are saturated with liberal thought or whose hearts are attuned to the values of the liberals, this is very attractive—attractive until men who are not under compulsion hold opinions or behave in a manner of which they strongly disapprove. Even then, they are not intellectually frustrated; they may, and do, point out that the opinions or behaviour of their opponents are inconsistent with the 'moral law', or the 'will of God'. But this does not in fact check their opponents' behaviour. The man who uses the 'moral law' or its equivalent to

---

[b]  On p. 15 of the copy text, Clark inserts a marginal note, 'A contradiction', to cover the two sentences beginning: 'But it does mean that . . .'.

restrain human behaviour may satisfy the canons of logical argument, but still fails to achieve an effective answer to the problem: how to restrain human conduct without compulsion. On the other hand, by eschewing compulsion, he is obliged to use some other method to persuade men to change either their values or their social organisation.

What Tocqueville believed in was the 'change of heart': that if men were appealed to they would, for example, perceive the injustice of economic inequality and would voluntarily surrender their surplus wealth to the poor. In the meantime there was to be no expropriation of the wealthy without their consent, nor any artificial assistance to the lower orders by the State, except in cases of dire necessity, for this would be compulsion, and compulsion was incompatible with liberty. These are exacting conditions. During his lifetime he saw no evidence that they would be fulfilled. In his own case a scrupulous observance of them led to withdrawal from human society. The pages that follow are written to prove that the pursuit of his ideal leads not to the good society of which he dreamed, but to isolation, to despair, to pessimism—and to the continuation of the conditions, the behaviour and the values which his ideal was designed to overcome.[c]

## Endnotes

[1] Review in *Gazette de France*, November 1835. This was the official organ of the Ultras.

[2] A. Rédier: *Comme disait M. de Tocqueville*, p. 8.

[3] Ibid., p. 2.

[4] Ibid., p. 5.

[5] One example of this is James Bryce: *The Predictions of Hamilton and de Tocqueville*.

[6] Professor Laski urged English publishers to do this in his review of J. P. Mayer's *Prophet of the Mass Age*. This review was written for the *New Statesman* in November 1939.

[7] A. Rédier: op. cit. in the Preface.

[8] H. J. Laski: 'Alexis de Tocqueville and Democracy' (see bibliography), p. 114.

[9] The work referred to is J. P. Mayer's *Prophet of the Mass Age*.

[10] Ibid., p. xvi.

---

[c] On p. 17 of the copy text, Clark inserts a marginal note: 'Pp. 13–17 need very careful revision'. This refers to the section beginning 'Now what Tocqueville saw very clearly . . .' (on p. 54) and continuing to the end of Chapter 1.

# CHAPTER II
## Man and Ideal

'A cool head and a logical mind . . . side by side with passions which overpower my will while leaving my reason free'.[1] Thus Tocqueville defined his personal problem. It is the age-old complaint of the intelligentsia: the mind jibs at or cowers before the generous or violent sentiments released by the heart. With Tocqueville the central problem is how to reconcile the sentiments of a lively heart with the conclusions of an active mind. For a man may dedicate his life to an ideal by which the dictates of the heart and the mind are both satisfied. Though the heart may be an unruly bedfellow, yet the mind may be strong enough to subdue it. But when the heart is reinforced by the passions roused in a time of troubles, then the promptings of the mind are swamped, conduct is determined by the stronger partner in the relationship. Certainly this was true of Tocqueville. By birth, education and temperament he was attracted to the aristocratic way of life—hence his passionate attachment to the aristocratic ideal of liberty. But his mind convinced him that the aristocratic way of life was doomed to extinction; so he became an intellectual convert to the democratic ideal—equality—and worked out an ideal for his contemporaries, a compromise between his personal tastes and his intellectual convictions which was to be the answer to the problems of his generation.

His affection for the aristocratic way of life is easily explained. The family background was favourable. Tocqueville's father was a count who enjoyed the confidence of Charles X and later earned the praise of Taine for his researches into the *ancien régime* and his reports on the prefecture of Metz. His mother too was a passionate adherent of the *ancien régime*, indeed so passionate that even in adolescence Tocqueville himself, the man with the 'cool head and the logical mind' could be reduced to tears of sympathy when his mother spoke of the execution of Louis XVI.[2] The ideals and stories of his parents had at least one permanent effect: even when he renounced their views he always wrote with warmth and affection of pre-revolutionary society, and was at pains to justify their behaviour to a suspicious generation. Hence the paradox of his last work, *L'Ancien Régime et la Révolution*, which contains both its best justification and its severest criticism. No wonder he was praised for his impartiality!

Curiously enough, the movement away from aristocratic society begins before he is openly critical of its assumptions. He is irritated with their way of life before he questions their values. The public service careers open to the members of his class bored him, while their leisure occupations—cards, dancing, drinking, gambling—roused his disgust and contempt.[3] To his intimate friends he wrote long letters lamenting the life he led, the society he frequented, and ending with the hope for new visions, new interests. Significantly enough, the adjustment made was a very minor one: there is no open revolt against or repudiation of the class in which he was born and educated. He seeks and finds men from his own class with the same interests. Not that noble birth becomes an indispensable qualification for friendship with him. There is a subtler, more indefinable quality required. A friend must be not only talented but also refined. Personal taste is more important than opinions. Thus, as we shall see again, the polite George Sand is warmly received, but the rude, crude Louis Blanqui ignored, although they held similar opinions.

And it was with this class, the refined intellectuals, that Tocqueville formed his strongest friendships. In France he corresponded regularly with Kergorlay, Beaumont, Corcelle—all members of the landed aristocracy; with Ampère, distinguished for his researches into the origins of German and Scandinavian poetry; with Gobineau, the author of *De l'Inégalité parmi les Races Humaines*; with Circourt, a contributor to the *Bibliothèque Universelle*, and the *Revue de Paris*. In England he corresponded with Lord Radnor, Sir George Cornwall Lewis, the historian of Rome; with Grote, the historian of Greece, and his wife; with John Stuart Mill, and Nassau Senior. It was this type of person that he lived with on his travels: in England with Lord Radnor or Sir George Lewis, or Grote or Nassau Senior; in America with the local men of importance. In 1851 when he was discussing the itinerary of his journey to Germany he insisted on living with a member of the Junker class.[4]

He turns to such men for the information he needs for his books. For knowledge on the effects of universal education, the importance of local government or the relations between the rich and poor in America, he consults Jared Sparks, a university professor.[5] To form an opinion on the influence of wealth in America he has a discussion with Mr Ingersoll, a distinguished lawyer and an ex-member of the legislature of Philadelphia. To ascertain the attitude of the Catholic Church to the American Constitution he consults Mr Powers, the Grand-Vicar for the Catholic Church in New York. In his American diary he carefully records the opinions of this class: he notes down the behaviour of other classes.[6] A man betrays his sympathies by the type of person he seeks out for information.

Tocqueville was peculiarly happy in such company. When isolated from congenial companions he sends out urgent, insistent invitations for them to visit him; after their departure he writes exquisite, wistful letters, recalling the pleasure of their stay and announcing his expectation of an early return. The published correspondence provides many illustrations of this point—indeed the correspondence leaves the impression that his small group of refined intellectuals was a mutual admiration society with Tocqueville as the chief recipient, and evidently not at all displeased by the arrangement. Royer-Collard told him that his work on America was the best contribution to the study of political institutions since the publication of *De l'Esprit des Lois*,[7] while John Stuart Mill was equally generous with his praise—'the beginning of a new era in the scientific study of politics'.[8] Whether these compliments were deserved is, for the moment, beside the point, the point being that Tocqueville enjoyed both the respect and the affection of the refined intellectuals of his generation, and was at ease in their company, or when cultivating the activities they valued.

At ease in <u>their</u> company, but curiously uncomfortable in the presence of other human beings. The number of times he asks himself how he is to behave towards other people indicates both the gulf between him and the rest, and the desperate attempts he made to bridge it. Yet these attempts were generally made with such bad grace that one's sympathies are, if anything, with those who were embarrassed or enraged by them. The story Beaumont tells of his attempts to be polite to the men with whom he usually voted in the Chamber of Deputies is typical of the gulf between the intention and the performance. 'You ask why Tocqueville joined the *Gauche* whom he despised . . . He allowed himself to be considered as a member of the *Gauche*, but I never could persuade him to be tolerably civil to them. Once, after I had been abusing him for his coldness to them, he shook hands with Ramorantin, then looked towards me for my applause, but I doubt whether he ever shook hands with him again.'[9]

There can be no doubt that this behaviour was an accurate indication of his real feelings. The bourgeoisie, he tells us in a calm mood, bore him profoundly,[10] while in less careful moods he often sneers at the 'stay-at-home petty bourgeois'.[11] Perhaps the gulf between ideal and behaviour is even more clearly defined in his relations with working men. The ideal which he set himself was stewardship and service: in their presence he was to be dignified, unaffected and yet not condescending or familiar; to please without giving offence.[12] How different was his behaviour whenever he actually came into contact with them! He travelled from England to France with some French peasants, and was horrified by them—'a detestable lot—noisy, ravening brutes, not fit to be at close quarters with a philosopher like me'.[13] These sentiments may be shocking to a generation taught to be sympathetic to working-class aspirations, and to explain their grossness by their living conditions. But Tocqueville lived at a time when the myth of a vicious social system had not replaced the myth of human viciousness as the explanation of evil. Nor was his reaction unique. Proudhon has told us of the 'inexpressible terror' which froze his soul when he saw the working classes in action,[14] while Guizot too 'shuddered', he said, before ' the mighty torrent ready to overflow and submerge the land'.[15] The sympathy with the people dried up as soon as they crossed the barrier between the study and the boulevard.

If we followed Tocqueville from the study to the boulevard, we should also notice the serenity disappear, anxiety creep over his face and with it the two emotions typical of the intelligentsia—contempt for the activities of others and despair for the future of the fine arts. Here too his sentiments are re-echoed by men with similar tastes— Chateaubriand's complaint that 'the times had become narrow-minded and coarse'[16] is typical. Nor are his criticisms excessively severe. Life in Paris was almost incredibly sordid in the decade preceding the revolution of 1848. The optimism of a Hugo, the cheerfulness and enthusiasm with which his characters sacrificed their lives for the coming Utopia, were exceptional. The disillusion of Flaubert's Frédéric, the despair of Balzac's Godéfroid in *L'Envers de l'Histoire Contemporaine* and the resignation of de Vigny's hero in *Servitude et Grandeur Militaires*—these were the typical responses of both young and old. Indeed it is tempting to accept Frédéric's explanation for his failure in life—the century in which he was born,[17] and ignore the weaknesses of character which deprived him of a faith to live by. Frédéric's fate does not excite pity or compassion; the age was unheroic and the adventurous spirits sublimated their dreams in fantasies about the heroic ages of the past: Chateaubriand's myth of the virile Christianity of the Middle Ages and de Vigny's myth of the heroes of Bonaparte.

The more familiar one becomes with the society under Louis Philippe, the more surprising it is that Tocqueville's condemnation of it was so mild, that he was able to remain almost unaffected by the *Zeitgeist* which unsettled so many. This is due not only to his distance from the society in which these problems were discussed, but also to his remoteness from the activities of the common man. The demi-monde which provided for the entertainment of the flotsam and jetsam of a large city never intruded on his consciousness. In 1848 he confessed he saw types on the streets whose existence he had never suspected before. Vice had no fascination for him—he does not mention it even in his most intimate correspondence—while excess in any form evoked horror and loathing.

His reticence on these subjects is intelligible and not very significant. What is revealing is his almost complete silence on the most acute social problem of the time—poverty. There was grinding poverty in the France of the bourgeois monarchy. In Paris men died in the streets of hunger every day, a fact which the wealthy explained as a disgusting attempt by the Carlists to discredit the régime of Louis Philippe.[18] In Lille 3,000 people were living in caves in conditions which stirred Adolphe Blanqui, a member of the Bourse, to compare their life with the animal kingdom to the advantage of the latter.[19] In the same city the infant mortality was appalling: out of 21,000 babies born only 300 reached the age of five.[20] The attitude adopted to this problem was by no means uniform. Some felt indignant; some, like Blanqui, were apprehensive and some, like Lamennais, anxious and puzzled. Was it not the weak and the meek who were begging for bread while the strong and the wicked were enjoying their ill-gotten gains?[21] True, not every one felt such poetic moral indignation with the distribution of wealth. But at least it excited the attention of most commentators.

Tocqueville himself was not entirely ignorant of these shocking conditions. He had read the pamphlets giving this information, and left the rough draft of an article embodying his main conclusions: 'De la Classe Moyenne et du Peuple'. Like Blanqui and many others he is alarmed, almost scared: 'once again the earth is trembling in Europe ... a revolutionary wind is in the air'.[22] But the striking point is the cause of his alarm. It is not the distressing scenes on the streets of Paris or the sight of the cave-dwellers on his journeys from Paris to his beloved Tocqueville, but the state of men's minds; in the upper and middle classes—apathy and preoccupation with material satisfactions; in the lower classes—immoral ideas. It is not what the eye can see and the ear can hear which tells him that there is something wrong in the state of Denmark. He knows 'by a kind of instinctive intuition which defies analysis' that 'the danger is real and serious'.[23] By a skilful transfer from the sordid descriptions of poverty to a vague but lofty diagnosis of the state of men's minds, he represses the painful ideas suggested by poverty and prepares his audience for his favourite solution—the spiritual purgative. He begs them to change the <u>spirit</u> of the government, because it is its spirit (not, mark you, poverty or corruption etc.) which is leading them to the abyss.[24]

No wonder the working classes were exasperated by the remedy of their social superiors—a lecture on their moral defects. What benefits would they have gained from this change of heart? Would it help to diminish the infant mortality rate in Lille? Would it provide adequate food and shelter for the paupers in town and country? Though we may be irritated by the attitude, especially the assumption of self-righteousness, we must not lose sight of its cause: the remote, sheltered life which Tocqueville led, in which material needs were so smoothly satisfied that any reference to them was considered distasteful and vulgar. If a member of his own class could not discipline his appetites, was not this a sign of moral weakness? Why not apply the same standard to the lower orders with their insistent demand for bread and still more bread? Even during the experiences of 1848 he was reluctant to admit that their material condition was the main cause of their conduct, while he never abandoned faith in the spiritual purgative as the panacea for social evils.*

An aristocrat with intellectual interests: that is the impression we have after a superficial review of his character and activities. An aristocrat, but too alert intellectually to put forward the arguments of his class to justify the superior position which he inherited; too conscientious to assume his social privileges without making some

---

* In a letter to Nassau Senior written in Paris in April 1848 he stated decisively his opinion on this issue. 'La révolution n'a point été amenée par la misère des classes ouvrières. Cette misère existait bien sur certains points, mais en général, on peut dire que dans aucun pays, dans aucun temps les classes ouvrières n'avaient été dans une meilleure condition qu'en France. Cela était surtout vrai de la classe ouvrière agricole . . . La crise qui tourmentait les ouvriers des grandes manufactures était passagère et, quoique assez intense, ne dépassait pas les bornes connues. Ce ne sont pas des besoins, ce, sont des idées qui ont amené ce grand bouleversement, des idées chimériques sur la condition relative de l'ouvrier et du capital, des théories exagérées sur le rôle que pouvait remplir le pouvoir social dans les rapports de l'ouvrier et du maître, des doctrines ultra-centralisantes qui avaient fini par persuader à des multitudes d'hommes qu'il ne dépendait que de l'Etat non seulement de les sauver de la misère, mais de leur donner l'aisance et le bien-être.' [The revolution was not

return. Even his social values, his attitude to his fellow-men, though redolent of feudal notions of status and stewardship, are never bluntly defended as the rewards of birth. Evidently he liked to be considered as an aristocrat who had abandoned his trappings to bring a message to the non-aristocratic world. He wrote tender letters to his nephews recommending these values. He was shocked when members of his class declined to follow his example. Moreover, this was the impression which he made on his friends—from which we infer that this behaviour was his ideal. Reeve's description of him makes this point very clearly: 'He belonged by nature to a chosen order of men. Indeed the extreme delicacy of his physical organisation, the fastidious refinement of his tastes, the exquisite charm of his manners, made him the very type of a high-bred gentleman; and if there were in him the outward signs of distinction, not less was he ennobled by the very soul of chivalry, by that purity, and simplicity of character which are the truest nobility, and by a combination of manly virtues with an almost feminine grace—qualities which Englishmen are wont to trace to an ideal perfection in the person of Sir Philip Sidney'.[25] Even if allowance be made for the circumstances in which this encomium was written—an obituary notice in the *Edinburgh Review*—Tocqueville was obviously very impressive in his chosen rôle and greatly appreciated by those with the same values.

It is difficult to reconcile this pen-portrait with the portraits preserved in the Château at Tocqueville. The face which greets the visitor to Tocqueville bears the marks of suffering, of conflict, as

---

brought about by the poverty of the working classes. There was certainly poverty in some respects, but in general it may be said that the condition of the working classes had never been better in any country or at any time, than in France. This was particularly true of the rural working class ... The crisis which afflicted the workers in the large factories was temporary, and although fairly acute, did not exceed known limits. It was not necessity but ideas which brought about this great upheaval, visionary ideas on the relative condition of the workers and capital, exaggerated theories of the role which might be played by social power in the relations between workers and their masters, ultra-centralist doctrines which had succeeded in persuading immense numbers of men that it depended on the state alone, not only to rescue them from want, but to give them affluence and material well-being.] *OE. C.* VI, 134.

well as grace and refinement. The intimate correspondence tells of *'passions ardentes'* [burning passions] which ruffled the serenity so sedulously cultivated. There is a plaintive note which is too insistent to be explained away as disapproval of the vulgar bourgeois or terror of the working classes. For Tocqueville was too sensitive to enjoy a serene and contented mind. As a youth he complained to his intimate friends of the agonies he experienced whenever he had to speak in public, of disgust with his performance as an orator, and the determination to master this discomfort.[26] As a man he resorted to the usual device of the sensitive—the social personality as a protective mask against the world. In public he was cold, reserved, even supercilious. This pose led to some odd misconceptions by casual acquaintances and observers. Heine stigmatised him as 'a man of intellect, not great of heart, who follows up the arguments of his logic to freezing point; his speeches too have a certain frosty brilliance like cut ice'[27]—a rare example of the fallibility of Heine's judgement on public men.

For Tocqueville's behaviour had all the symptoms of a man endowed with a very warm heart as well as an active mind. There is enough warmth in any one of his letters to Kergorlay or to Eugène Stoffels to thaw the ice in all his public statements. Indeed the affection of his intimate friends is his one compensation for the pain suffered as soon as he moved from the warm, sympathetic environment of his own circle to the cold, hostile world. The extent of his dependence upon their affection is reflected in the melancholy which he experienced on their death. The thought with which he eased his anguish—that it was better to die than to endure the sufferings of this world[28]—indicates how slender were the threads binding him to this existence and the strength of the desire to find refuge from its slings and arrows.

One more symptom of his sensitiveness before we notice the refuges he sought: he was almost ludicrously apprehensive. His first reactions to an environment generally went beyond astonishment and wonder. The opening remark in a letter from England portrays the tension, the pent-up emotions roused by other customs: 'The state of religion in England seems to me such as to give rise to considerable anxiety'.[29] And because he was apprehensive, he was in-

ordinately gullible if the stories told him reinforced the anxieties
he entertained. In 1833 we find him touring Ireland with Beaumont
—so that year his friends received Jeremiads on the future of that
country, on imminent, violent and bloody revolutions. By chance
another distinguished traveller, William Makepeace Thackeray,
visited the same districts in 1842, and found the peasants still
chuckling over the tall stories they had spun to the credulous
Frenchman. Thackeray rightly insists on the danger of making predictions on purely anecdotal evidence.[30]

It would of course be absurd to suggest that all Tocqueville's
ideas were based on evidence collected in this way. But the story
does suggest that he did not enjoy the peace of mind necessary for
the digestion of the information he collected. One writer has suggested that he had a ruminating mind, that he chewed the cud of
his reflections.[31] Perhaps he did—sometimes. But at other times he
was like a young heifer let loose in a paddock of lucerne who, left
alone, immediately gorged herself and then stood inflated, unwell,
feeling that something must be done immediately or the world
would blow up. But then it was she, and not necessarily the world,
who had the stomach-ache! And he wrote his books when experi-
encing this emotional tension—what he called his '*terreur religieuse*'
[religious dread].[32]

Fantasy is a very soothing pastime for those who find the world
unbearable, especially if the mind does not jib at the pictures which
the imagination wafts gently over the stream of consciousness. And
fantasy was one of his refuges. He dreamt of a life in which he could
play a more active and satisfying role, but the 'cool head' posed the
awkward question: where? He liked to think that men had not
always been so corrupt, so crude, so vulgar; that, for example, the
men who made the French Revolution acted on higher motives than
those which influenced his contemporaries.[33] But again the 'cool
head' disagreed. Reason is a kill-joy! Still, there was the world of
make-believe. In 1836 he told Royer-Collard that he had built in his
imagination an ideal city inhabited by perfect men, to be used as a
haven from this world.[34] And twenty years' experience as a writer
and a public man did not diminish the need for such a myth. Three
years before his death he wrote of the pain of living in a world

which was such a poor substitute for that ideal creation in which his spirit loved to dwell.[35] Because his mind passed easily from reality to make-believe, especially if the fantasy was not too repugnant to the 'cool head', his books were '*rêveries*' rather than 'fact', reflections more than accounts—reflections which will excite and inspire the reader unless he remembers that the man who wrote them was also searching for a comforter.

A comforter to appease the pangs of doubt—this was perhaps his strongest desire; for doubt was, in his experience, the most painful evil in this world, worse even than death.[36] So he feverishly studied the subjects which claim to give an answer—religion and philosophy. Study of the latter irritated him, superficially because of its method, which he called casuistry and logomachy, fundamentally because of its fruits—scepticism, a barren and uninviting creed for a man of his temperament.[37] He wanted a guide to conduct, a re-assurance, not the damping conclusion that man was never sure of anything. Yet if his 'heart' was distressed by the conclusions of philosophy, his mind was just as reluctant to assent to the fundamental doctrines of religion. At the age of seventeen he lost his religious faith, and does not seem to have regained it until shortly before his death.[38] Still he appears to have had a very strong will to believe; what was perhaps even stronger was his conviction of the <u>necessity</u> to believe, a conviction based on observation of the consequences of unbelief. Because he recommends religion to his contemporaries, we infer that he was afraid of the unleashing of the 'burning passions' in other people—passions which he believed in his own case were subdued by a strong mind.

The strong mind—the jar to his inner peace, the snag which prevented full assent to his desires. For religion not only provided the comforter, but also an assurance that his personal tastes were right. Christian teaching condemned the material and extolled the spiritual pleasures; Tocqueville adored the soul and wanted it to dominate the life of man.[39] For this reason he approved of Plato, and what he was trying to do—'his consistently spiritual and lofty aspirations'.[40] Machiavelli, on the other hand, distressed him. He did not like to believe that men were as he portrayed them.[41] His heart was with the men and the religions which preached asceticism, even mortification of the flesh. (In parentheses it may be noticed that there is no evidence that he practised any of the disciplines recommended by those teachers who roused such sympathetic responses in his breast.)

Still he could not accept their doctrines; the mind raised insuperable objections. Man had a body as well as a soul; the angel was enclosed by the beast. Every philosophy, every religion which neglected entirely one of these two entities might produce some extraordinary examples of human achievement, but it would never have a powerful influence on the mass of mankind. Expediency dictated a compromise between the two extremes of conduct, a middle road which would lead humanity to neither Sodom nor the Madonna, for the majority of men would not pursue one to the exclusion of the other, or if they did, Sodom and not the Madonna would be their choice. So why be shocked by the honest materialism of the bourgeois, his lust for filthy lucre? Why not accept it as part of human nature? This was not the language of the heart; he groaned inwardly, he told Kergorlay, whenever he assented to this position.[42] The curious thing is that a man sheltered from the rough and tumble life of the masses, and with such strong affections for the life of the spirit, should have reached such a common-sense position on a question which, because it intimately affects human behaviour, incites men to excess and bombast. But perhaps in our zeal to present the secret affections of his heart, we have not stressed sufficiently the strength of their severest critic—his own mind.

If his emotional sympathies alone had determined his ideals, Tocqueville would have been a follower of the Catholic idealists, de Bonald and de Maistre. The ideal of the bourgeois—the accumulation of wealth—was too repugnant to excite his sympathies, let alone his approval. If usury was the compass by which the bourgeois guided his life, Tocqueville would have endured the inconveniences of a more primitive method of navigation rather than be assisted by such a distasteful instrument. The ideal of the working classes—material well-being as the *sine qua non* of happiness—is condemned because of the importance attached to wealth. There is a Gilbertian situation in his repudiation of their ideal. Tocqueville had wealth, but denied its importance; working men lacked it, and extolled its value. Yet the very men who are contemptuous of the 'materialists' become most indignant when told that their wealth must be shared with other men, if their ideals are to be realised. Idealists are generally the most tenacious defenders of private property, even when the motives they cite to justify their behaviour are not tainted by the material gains they are making. Indeed the heart is often the pocket's best employee.

With Tocqueville, however, the heart was shocked both by the bourgeois' habit of unashamedly declaring his pocket to be his ideal, and by the working man's determination to acquire the bourgeois' wealth either by violence or by an appeal to the latter's better self. But with the Catholic idealists these emotional sympathies and antipathies were defended as evidence of a higher 'nature'. They too were contemptuous of the vulgar pursuits of the bourgeois. More important: they were sceptical of the pleasures to be enjoyed in this world, and invited their followers to withdraw from it and concentrate on the unseen world where true joys were to be found. Yet Tocqueville repudiated their ideal, not because he was not attracted to it, but because it was repugnant to his mind. It is high time we noticed the qualities of this mind, and the conclusions he reached by exercising it.

Perhaps its most striking quality is its curiosity: the whole field of human experience is perused with an inquiring eye. He wanted to know the causes of events, the sources of human action, the motives which have governed the actions both of himself and his neighbours. We know this not only from the questions he addresses to other people, but also by the surprise expressed whenever he met other human beings who were not interested in these questions. As a youth he spent some time with the Beaumont family and was struck by the lively interest they took in the growth of a tree, the raising of a crop or the hatching of a brood, and the fact that their interest did not go beyond observation: they asked how? and never why? And it was the answer to the 'why' which was the most important point for him.[43]

At least it is the hope of finding an answer which is the motive for the inquiry. When the prospect of an answer is remote, or the answer is unpleasant, interest flags; the mind wanders, or assents to opinions for which the evidence is not too weak. The empirical analysis is never sustained beyond the point where doubt or scepticism are the only positions compatible with the evidence. This is the explanation for his initial interest in philosophy, and the loss of interest as soon as he perceived that the answers he was looking for were simply not there. Because his mind wobbled at the critical points in its search for the *deus ex machina*, and accepted certain doctrines of faith, he was apt to resort to the same method when baffled by problems of human behaviour. To explain the belief in equality prevalent in certain classes, he introduces the abstract concept of man's innate '*goût*' [taste] for equality; he also explains centralisation by the '*instinct naturel*' [natural instinct]. We shall see how this tended not only to make his thought confused, but also distracted his attention from the empirical causes of the problems he was discussing.

One other pointer to the type of mind he possessed: at school he was a poor student of the precise subjects—Latin, mathematics and the sciences—but brilliant in the humanities, winning the Honours prize for rhetoric and two other first prizes.[44] Where the mind could wander freely from idea to idea without the discipline of reality, he was at his best. The curious thing is that it could, at the same time, call a halt whenever he crossed the slender frontier between reality and the pleasing lands of make-believe. For the criterion by which his mind judged an ideal was not the strength of his sympathy with it, but the stern pragmatic test: did it work? And if the ideal did not satisfy this standard he rejected it, even if he felt the strongest emotional sympathy with it. Kergorlay's ideal of the mortification of the flesh is rejected because it did not satisfy this standard—it was unattractive to the great mass of mankind. And it was the 'cool head' which converted him to the ideal of democracy —a conversion in opposition to the dictates of his heart.[d]

---

[d]  On p. 37 of the copy text, Clark inserts a marginal note, 'Amend', to cover the section beginning 'Kergorlay's ideal . . .' to the end of the paragraph. These revisions were made (in manuscript) and have been incorporated in this edition.

There is simply no other explanation for his belief in democracy after the American journey. He was certainly not a believer before he departed. The one surviving written statement of his opinions is a strong indictment of its ideals and institutions.[45] Nor was he attracted by the strange customs and ways of life of a people who were making some attempt to observe the principles of equality and fraternity. On the contrary, he was not only surprised but also unwilling to abandon the social manners of his own class. The activities which he believed to be the essence of civilisation were ignored by the Americans: there were no literature, no oratory, no fine arts—not even castles! Their social customs too were queer: uniform dress, uniform behaviour, uniform opinions—dull and drab after the diversity of Europe.[46] Everyone shook hands, irrespective of class or creed. Even the District Attorney shook hands with members of the lower orders. True, some were rich and some poor, but the wealthy behaved to the poor as though they were their social equals. Tipping was not practised because it might attach the stigma of inferiority to the recipient. Inn-keepers lived on a footing of social equality with the patrons; they sat at the same table, served the meal and joined in the conversation.[47]

Most of these observations are copied into his journal without comment, but though Tocqueville spent a great deal of time recommending people to adopt the ideal of democracy, he never once recommended them to copy American social customs. The apostle of democracy was never very fond of the manners of democrats. The heart recorded embarrassment, but the mind required more substantial evidence before it echoed the heart's repudiation. Here was a society with an ideal and institutions which his European mentors had taught him would produce anarchy, economic ruin and unhappiness. But had it? Until he had a satisfactory answer to these questions, judgement must be suspended. The touchstone will be his own observations and the information he can collect from the social and political leaders of the country. The first conclusion is that the Americans are both prosperous and happy—'that this nation is one of the happiest on earth'.[48] And the second is that the arguments used against democracy in Europe have simply not been proved true: democracy did work. The religious authorities were convinced that it did not cause a decrease in the number of believers, nor a challenge to their faith. The educational authorities assured him that universal education did not intensify the antagonism or envy of the poor for the rich. True, the evidence on the ability of the people to choose the wisest and best men as their leaders was not very reassuring, but the Americans felt confident that improvements in education would produce the desired results.[49]

Even by the middle of the journey, the tone of his letters home begins to change. The society with the odd social customs has a message for Europe: democracy does work. The mind has subdued the protests of the heart, subdued but not destroyed them. For it is, at most, an intellectual conversion. There is no dramatic repudiation of the old ways of life, no decision to forsake all and preach the ideal of democracy to France and Europe. In temperament and behaviour he remained substantially the same—aloof, remote and unsociable. Even in 1848 he objected to the use of democratic language when referring to politicians: *citoyen* smelt strongly of the type of fraternity practised in America! Nor did he deliberately cultivate bourgeois society, join their political clubs or contribute to their journals. He became an 'arm-chair' democrat, or, to put it bluntly, he did not practise the rites of his religion. Still the impression made on his mind was profound: even twenty-seven years of public life, spent mostly in an undemocratic environment, did not efface the conclusions formed—'As for the main body of my ideas . . . I would not change one of them'.[50]

His temperament did not change; and it was the difference between the affections of the heart and the conclusions of the mind which determined his ideal. His heart spontaneously and warmly accepted the three ideals in the aristocratic creed—the supremacy of the soul, social inequality, and liberty. But the mind rejected the first as chimerical and the second as impossible in a society where belief in social equality was almost universal. Both heart and mind approved of liberty, though, as we shall see presently, the mind was sceptical of its appeal to any but the very few. On the other hand there were objections to the three ideals in the democratic creed:

private judgement, equality and liberty. Private judgement meant in practice either apathy or scepticism, pretexts for the evasion of all moral laws. And though the mind could find no arguments to refute scepticism, the heart was so uneasy as to the consequences of un-belief that toleration of private judgement, though sound in theory, was personally repugnant to him. Equality too raised the same dilemma: the heart disapproved, but the mind knew that men could be prosperous in an egalitarian society: more, that most men wanted social equality.

To liberty, both heart and mind responded warmly, but the mind was suspicious of the democratic conception of liberty: was it not used for the wrong reasons—the accumulation of wealth—and not for the reasons which appealed so strongly to him—the culti-vation of the mind? Between 1831 and 1835 his mind ruminated on these problems. In the latter year he offered the fruits of his reflec-tion to the world in the first two volumes of *De la Démocratie en Amérique*. In the next year he wrote to Mill a plain statement of his ideal—liberty and equality. Liberty was the child of his heart—*'j'aime avec passion la liberté'* [I love liberty passionately]—but equal-ity was the child of his mind—*'un goût de tête'* [an intellectual taste]. And the discussion of these two ideals makes it abundantly clear that his liberty is the product of his *'instinct aristocratique'* [aristo-cratic instinct] while equality is the result of the 'cool head'.*

Even the arguments used to justify his belief in these ideals reveal the kind of attachment he felt for them. Affection for liberty

---

* Tocqueville himself was aware of the difference in the reasons for his affection for lib-erty and for equality.

  *J'ai pour les institutions démocratiques un goût de tête, mais je suis aristocratique par l'instinct, c'est à dire que je méprise et crains la foule.*

  *J'aime avec passion la liberté, la légalité, le respect des droits, mais non la démocra-tie. Voilà le fond de l'âme. Je hais la démagogie, l'action désordonnée des masses, leur intervention violente et mal éclairée dans les affaires, les passions envieuses des basses classes, les tendances irréligieuses. Voilà le fond de l'âme.*

  *Je ne suis ni du parti révolutionnaire, ni du parti conservateur. Mais, cependant et après tout, je tiens plus au second qu'au premier. Car je diffère du second plutôt par les moyens que par la fin, tandis que je diffère du premier tout à la fois par les moyens et la fin.*

  *La liberté est la première de mes passions. Voilà ce qui est vrai.'*

is evidence of the greatness of a man's soul: only the men with '*grands coeurs*' [great hearts] are sincerely attached to it. Liberty excites the noble sentiments in man, distracts the mind from the petty thoughts of everyday life, raises man from the beasts to the angels. For liberty is '*un goût sublime*' [a sublime taste] intelligible to the 'great hearts' whom God has prepared to receive it, but incomprehensible to '*âmes médiocres*' [mediocre souls].[51] How different from equality, '*ce goût dépravé*' [this depraved taste], which excites the souls of the mediocre, and terrifies the great![52] Yet, despite the ill-concealed personal disapproval, he urges his contemporaries to accept equality. The arguments are directed not to the many, who were already practising believers, but to the few, the 'great hearts' like himself, to whom the ideal was distasteful. The discussion implies sympathy with and understanding of their feelings, and enjoins them to allow reason to prevail.

The interesting thing is that he was evidently not convinced by the empirical arguments. Men wanted equality; the history of the last eight hundred years was the gradual evolution of equality.[53] Was this sufficiently persuasive? Perhaps the stubborn would be unimpressed. So the will of God is invoked to convince the sceptical that resistance to the movement is tantamount to rebellion against God.[54] At the same time the doubters are comforted with the assurance of the goodness of God's intentions for mankind.[55] Yet though God is introduced to strengthen the argument, [Tocqueville] never uses moral arguments to justify his belief in equality. The reader is

---

[For democratic institutions I have an intellectual taste but I am aristocratic by instinct, that is to say, I despise and fear the multitude.

I passionately love liberty, legality, respect for legal rights, but not democracy—in my heart of hearts.

I hate demagogy, the unruly action of the masses, their violent and ill-informed interference in affairs, the envious passions of the lower orders, and irreligious tendencies—in my heart of hearts.

I belong neither to the revolutionary party nor to the conservative party. But all things considered, I tend more to the latter than the former. For I differ from the latter more as to means than ends, whereas I differ from the former both as to means and ends.

My foremost passion is liberty. And that is the truth of the matter.] Quoted in A. Rédier: op. cit. p. 48.

not told he ought to believe in equality because it is more just than inequality. Even the assent of God is not used as evidence for the justness of the ideal. Personal sympathies must be subordinated to the *fait accompli*. After all, the enthusiasts for equality were the 'mediocre souls', while the conception he had of liberty was incompatible with the behaviour of the disciples of equality.

For liberty was not permission to do anything that was pleasing. Vulgar behaviour, pursuit of wealth, violence, even anarchy may be pleasing. But Tocqueville did not approve of them, and his conception of liberty provides no justification for such behaviour. Men who do only what is pleasing do not experience the noble sentiments excited by true liberty: they become, on the contrary, inferior to themselves.[56] Nor is liberty to be loved because of the material benefits it bestows on its followers. Liberty generally brings comfort, well-being, even wealth in the long run, but at times it brings hardship and poverty. Then the men who valued only its material benefits would discard it, and embrace any creed which guaranteed their material possessions.[57] But such behaviour would not occur if they were faithful to his conception of liberty—'to do all that is good and just without compulsion'.[58] By 'good' he means the teaching of the Catholic Church. At least this was his final position. The scepticism of the majority, in some cases their suspicion and hostility to the Church made it unlikely that many would accept the authority he was recommending. But the objections to the alternative authority—self-interest—were insuperable: by this criterion he could justify his own behaviour, but so could the bourgeois. Besides, he agreed substantially with the values of the Church, while the assurance that in obeying its teaching he was following the commandments of God was very attractive to him.[e]

The interpretation of the phrase 'without compulsion' is equally pleasing to his personal sympathies. All determinist doctrines angered him. Some men asserted that all human actions were determined by '*une force insurmontable et inintelligente, que naît des*

---

[e]  On p. 43 of the copy text, Clark inserts a marginal note, 'Amend', to cover the section beginning 'At least this was his final position . . .'.

*événements antérieurs, de la race, du sol ou du climat'* [an insurmountable and unreasoning force born of anterior events, of race, soil or climate]. But these were the opinions of cowards and liars: cowards, because weak men used them to justify their excesses; liars, because men were neither completely independent nor completely enslaved. Within the limits defined by God they had free choice.[59] The implication was that within these limits the individual must decide for himself without compulsion. To use this liberty, with which they were endowed by their Creator, men must have rights—the rights to express their opinions in speech or in writing, to associate with other men, to have a voice in the decisions of their government. Any infringement of these rights is a negation of liberty. The proper use of these rights or liberties is secured in the second half of the definition. They shall be used to do what is good and just.

Belief in true liberty was a sign of superior taste. Belief in equality was a sign of correct historical insight. In the evolution of an egalitarian society, there were three distinct phases. First, there was the attack on privileges conferred by birth. In America this phase had been completed before his arrival—'the last vestiges of rank and hereditary distinctions have been destroyed'.[60] In England, too, wealth—*'chose aquérable'* [which can be acquired]—and not birth, determined one's social class.[61] The abolition of hereditary distinctions was the forerunner of the second phase—inequality of wealth but equality of opportunity. In America, for example, everyone had the same educational opportunities although the income levels of the parents differed considerably.[62]* In England, men tolerated the extremes of wealth and poverty so long as they believed that they

---

* Even in America there was not equality of opportunity. All children received primary education, but wealth, not talent, determined the right to proceed to secondary education. In one passage Tocqueville asserts there was equality of opportunity: *'les intelligences, tout en restant inégales ... trouvent à leur disposition des moyens égaux'* [although not all endowed with equal intelligence, all have equal [educational] opportunities]. (*De la Démocratie en Amérique* I, p. 84). Yet in the same work he points out that only very few could afford to give their children a higher education: *'l'instruction primaire y est à la portée de chacun; l'instruction supérieure n'y est presque à la portée de personne* [in America primary education is within the reach of all, but higher education is within the reach of hardly anyone] (ibid., I, p. 83).

were not disqualified by birth or law from amassing a fortune.[63] The third phase would be the introduction of economic equality, mentioned in a prophecy made by de Tocqueville in 1835—'Is it to be expected that after destroying feudalism and defeating the kings, democracy will draw back in the face of the bourgeoisie and the wealthy? Will it stop, now that it has grown so strong and its opponents so weak?'[64] By the forties, the demands of the socialists were adequate evidence for the statement. The term 'equality' means, then, any one of these three phases.

The reader is prepared for the major recommendation not, as in the case of liberty, by a eulogy of its charm and the subtle insinuation that sympathy with the ideal is proof of being a superior soul, but by a sketch of what has in fact occurred and what is most likely to happen in the future. The two arguments are: accept equality even if you do not like it, because there will be equality, and secondly, accept 'the social condition [equality] which Providence imposes on them'.[65] At least, those were the reasons by which he persuaded himself to believe in the ideal. If we read the preface to *De la Démocratie en Amérique*, it appears that he is prepared to repress the strong personal distaste for an egalitarian society, that as far as he was concerned society would and should pass from the second phase, equality of opportunity, to the third, economic equality; that resistance to this development was a sign either of stupidity or rebellion against God.

But alas, he can only approve of an egalitarian society which provides conditions compatible with his conception of liberty. These were so exacting that we doubt whether any society could change from phase two to phase three without infringing them. First, the motives for the change must not be purely materialist—a standard which, by itself, excluded the bourgeois and the worker from participation in the movement; second, no individual must be compelled to share his wealth with other men, nor must any individual receive assistance from the government. These principles assume a 'change of heart' in the rich and exclude all forms of government control of the economic well-being of members of the community. The egalitarian society must conform to the standards prescribed by liberty; the tastes of the aristocrat are more important than the 'intellectual taste'.

One more observation before we conclude the chapter. The changes to the constitution of the July Monarchy must be few and gradual. The radical sentiments implicit in the ideal are whittled away in the programme for action which he drew up for his friends and admirers.*ᶠ Besides, his aristocratic aloofness made political

---

\* The most detailed statement of his programme is contained in a letter to E. Stoffels written in October 1836:

'. . . *Quelle est la fin? Ce que je veux, ce n'est pas une république, mais une monarchie héréditaire. Je l'aimerais même mieux légitime qu'élue ainsi que celle que nous avons, parce qu'elle serait plus forte surtout à l'extérieur. Ce que je veux, c'est un gouvernement central énergique dans la sphère de son action. L'énergie du pouvoir central est bien plus nécessaire chez un peuple démocratique où la force sociale est disséminée que dans une aristocratie. D'ailleurs notre situation en Europe nous fait une loi impérieuse de ce qui devrait être une chose de choix. Mais je veux que ce pouvoir central ait une sphère nettement tracée; qu'il se mêle de ce qui rentre nécessairement dans ses attributions, et non de tout en général, et qu'il soit toujours subordonné, quant à sa tendance, à l'opinion publique et au pouvoir législatif qui la représente. Je crois que le pouvoir central peut être revêtu de très grandes prérogatives, être énergique et puissant dans sa sphère, et en même temps les libertés provinciales être très développées. Je pense qu'un gouvernement de cette espèce peut exister, et qu'en même temps la majorité de la nation peut se mêler elle-même de ses propres affaires, que la vie politique peut arriver à être répandue presque partout; l'exercice direct ou indirect des droits politiques très étendu. Je veux que les principes généraux du gouvernement soient libéraux, que la part la plus large possible soit laissée à l'action des individus, à l'initiative personnelle. Je crois que toutes ces choses sont compatibles; bien mieux, je suis profondément convaincu qu'il n'y aura jamais d'ordre et de tranquillité que quand on sera parvenu à les combiner.*

*Quant aux moyens: avec tous ceux qui admettent que c'est le but vers lequel on doit tendre, je me montre aussitôt très conciliant. Je suis le premier à admettre qu'il faut marcher lentement, avec précaution, avec légalité. Ma conviction est que nos institutions actuelles suffisent pour arriver au résultat que j'ai en vue. Loin donc de vouloir qu'on viole les lois, je professe un respect presque superstitieux pour les lois. Mais je veux que les lois tendent peu à peu et graduellement vers le but que je viens d'indiquer, au lieu de faire des efforts impuissants et dangereux pour rebrousser chemin. Je veux que le gouvernement prépare lui-même les moeurs et les usages à ce qu'on se passe de lui dans bien des cas où son intervention est encore nécessaire ou invoquée sans nécessité. Je veux qu'on introduise les citoyens dans la vie publique à mesure qu'on les croit capables d'y être utiles, au lieu de chercher à les en écarter à tout prix. Je veux enfin que l'on sache où l'on veut aller, et qu'on y marche prudemment au lieu de procéder à l'aventure, comme on n'a guère cessé de faire depuis vingt ans . . . En résumé, je conçois nettement l'idéal d'un gouvernement qui n'a rien de révolutionnaire ni d'agité outre mesure et que je crois possible de donner à notre pays, mais d'un autre côté, je conçois aussi bien que*

*personne qu'un pareil gouvernement (qui n'est du reste que l'extension de celui que nous avons), pour s'établir, a besoin de moeurs, d'habitudes, de lois qui n'existent pas encore, et qui ne peuvent être introduites que lentement et avec de grandes précautions . . .'*
Tocqueville, 5 October 1836

'. . . What is the ultimate goal? What I want is not a republic but a hereditary monarchy. I would actually prefer one based on legitimacy to an elected monarchy such as the one we have, because it would be stronger, particularly in external relations. What I want is a central government operating energetically within its sphere of action. Energy on the part of the central power is far more necessary in a democratic nation, where social power is widely distributed, than in an aristocracy. Moreover, our situation within Europe renders imperative what should be a matter of choice. But I want the sphere of action of this central power to be clearly defined; I want it to deal only with matters strictly within its jurisdiction, and not with general policy; to be always subordinated, in matters of policy, to public opinion as represented by the legislature. I believe that this central power may be vested with great prerogatives, may be energetic and powerful within its sphere, while at the same time the liberties enjoyed by the provinces are also highly developed. I believe that a government of this kind can exist at the same time as the majority of the people go about their own business; that political life may eventually extend almost universally; that the direct or indirect exercise of political rights may be very widespread. I want the general principles of government to be very liberal, and the largest possible share in government to be left to individuals, to personal initiatives. I believe that all these things are compatible; moreover, I am profoundly convinced that order and tranquillity will never prevail until we have succeeded in combining them.

As to means: I am more than ready to meet halfway all those who admit that this is the goal we should aim for. I am the first to admit that we should proceed slowly, with caution and legality. It is my conviction that our present institutions are adequate to achieve the result I have in mind. Far from endorsing any violation of the laws, I profess an almost superstitious respect for the law. But I want the laws to move gradually, bit by bit, towards the goal I have indicated, instead of making ineffectual and dangerous efforts to turn back the clock. I would like the government itself to bring in customs and usages making the government redundant in many cases where its intervention is still necessary or is needlessly invoked. I want the citizens to be introduced into public life when and as they are believed capable of participating usefully, instead of seeking to exclude them from it at all costs.

Finally, I want us to know where we want to go, and to advance prudently towards our goal, instead of proceeding haphazardly, as we have done almost without exception for the past twenty years.

To sum up, I clearly envisage the ideal of a government which is neither revolutionary nor over-restive, and which I believe it possible to give our country. On the other hand I realise as clearly as anybody that in order to establish a government of this kind (which is simply an extension of the one we now have) requires customs, habits and laws which do not yet exist and which can be introduced only slowly and with great caution'. *OE. C. V*, 434–6.

On p. 47 of the copy text, Clark inserts a marginal note: 'Besides, his aristocratic aloofness made political action so distasteful and painful to him that he does not seem to have gone beyond the stage of urging his ideas in books and speeches'.

action so distasteful and painful to him, that he does not seem to have gone beyond the stage of urging his ideas in books and speeches. But in 1836 it is not possible to accuse him of insincerity, to say that he did not want the changes which his ideal entailed. What is clear is his doubt as to the capacity or desire of all to pursue his ideal. And the chief doubt is: if men possess the liberties will they use them to do what is good and just? His answer to this question will be the subject of the next chapter.[g]

## Endnotes

1 *'La tête froide et l'esprit raisonneur … et à côté de cela … des passions … domptant ma volonté en laissant libre ma raison'*. *OE. C.* V, 420. Letter to E. Stoffels, Philadelphia, 18.10.1831.

2 Mayer, op. cit., p. 3.

3 *OE. C.* V, 300–2. Letter to Kergorlay, Versailles 23.7.1827.

4 *OE. C.* V, 385–6. Letter to Kergorlay, Bonn, 2.7.1854.

5 *'Cahiers'* [Notebooks] of American journey in archives at Tocqueville.

6 Ibid.

7 An unpublished letter by R. Collard to one of his friends, 15.2.1836.

8 An unpublished letter by J. S. Mill to Tocqueville, 11.5.1840.

9 M. C. M. Simpson, 'Correspondence and Conversations of A. de Tocqueville with Nassau William Senior from 1834–59', II, 264–5.

10 Quoted in E. Faguet, *Politiques et Moralistes du 19ᵉ siècle*, p. 67.

11 *'petit pot-au-feu bourgeois'*. *OE. C.* VII, 180. Letter to Beaumont, Tocqueville, 9.8.1840.

12 Louis de Loménie: 'Publicistes Modernes de la France' (in *Revue des Deux Mondes*, 15.5.1859, p. 420).

13 *'une race détestable, animaux rangeurs et bruyants, dont le voisinage ne convient pas à un philosophe comme moi.'* *OE. C.* VI, 69. Letter to Reeve, 24.7.1837.

14 F. Jellinek: *Paris Commune of 1871*, p. 130.

15 M. Guizot: 'Democracy in France, January 1849', p. 10.

16 *'le siècle était devenu étroit et grossier'*. L. Blanc: *Histoire de Dix Ans*, III, 3.

17 G. Flaubert: *L'Education Sentimentale*, p. 570.

18 H. Heine: *Sämmtliche Werke* VIII, p. 136.

---

g On p. 47 of the copy text, beneath the concluding sentence of the chapter, Clark inserts the following: '*It would be interesting to examine more closely his [Tocqueville's] work as a deputy and a minister to test this opinion. My impression when reading the Tocqueville papers was that he was temperamentally suited to analysing what <u>ought</u> to be done—in penal reform, colonial reform, social conditions etc.—but unsuited to translating his ideas into action. There is a summary of his behaviour as a politician in R. P. Marcel: *Essai Politique sur Alexis de Tocqueville*'.

19   A. Blanqui: *Des Classes Ouvrières en France pendant l'année 1848*, p. 100.

20   Ibid., pp. 101–2.

21   M. Lamennais: *Paroles d'un Croyant*, p. 31.

22   *'le sol tremble de nouveau en Europe . . . un vent de révolutions . . . est dans l'air.'* *OE. C.* IX, 534. Speech in Chamber of Deputies, 27.1.1848.

23   *'par une sorte d'intuition instinctive qui ne peut s'analyser . . . le danger est réel et sérieux'.* Ibid.

24   Ibid., 535.

25   H. Reeve, 'The remains of Alexis de Tocqueville', *Edinburgh Review*, Vol. CXIII, January 1861, p. 440.

26   *OE. C.* V, 300–2. Letter to Kergorlay, Versailles, 23.7.1827.

27   'Ein Mann von kopf, der wenig Herz hat, und bis zum Gefrierpunkt die Argumente seiner Logik verfolgt; auch haben seine Reden einen gewissen frostigen Glanz wie geschnittenes Eis'. H. Heine: *Sämmtliche Werke* X, 244–5.

28   *OE. C.* VII, 60. Letter to Baron de Tocqueville, Boston, 10.9.1831.

29   'L' *état de la religion en Angleterre me semble de nature à causer quelque inquiétude.'* *OE. C.* VIII, 323. 'Voyage en Angleterre', 25 August 1833.

30   W. M. Thackeray: 'Irish Sketch Book' in same volume as 'Yellow Plush Papers' (London) p. 237.

31   Review of *OE. C.* VIII in *Pall Mall Gazette*, 19 May 1865, p. 11.

32   *De la Démocratie en Amérique* I, 8.

33   Unpublished letter by Tocqueville to R. Collard, undated, but probably written in 1836.

34   Ibid.

35   *OE. C.* VI, 350. Letter to Mme Swetchine, Tocqueville, 20.10.1856.

36   *OE. C.* VI, 350. Letter to Corcelle, Tocqueville, 1.8.1850.

37   *OE. C.* V, 356–7. Letter to Kergorlay, Tocqueville, 8.8.1838.

38   A. Rédier: op. cit., pp. 38–9.

39   *OE. C.* V, 326. Letter to Kergorlay, Baden, 5.8.1836.

40   *'son aspiration continuellement spiritualiste et haute.'* Ibid.

41   Ibid.

42   Ibid.

43   G. W. Pierson: *Tocqueville and Beaumont in America*, p. 21.

44   A. Rédier: op. cit., pp. 38–9.

45   Ibid., p. 92.

46   *OE. C.* VII, 70. Letter to Comtesse de Grancey, New York, 10.10.1831.

47   Notebooks of American journey.

48   *'que ce peuple-ci est un des plus heureux qu' il y ait au monde'.* *OE. C.* VII, 23. Letter to the Comte de Tocqueville, Sing Sing, 3.6.1831.

49   Notebooks of American journey.

50   *'Quant au gros de mes idées . . . je n'y changerais rien.'* *OE. C.* VI, 288. Letter to Beaumont, Compiègne, 21.2.1855.

51   *OE. C.* IV, 248. *L'Ancien Régime.*

52   *OE. C.* I, 86. *De la Démocratie en Amérique.*

53   Ibid., I, 7.

54   Ibid., I, 8.

55   Ibid.

56   *OE. C.* IX, 421. From Speech in the Chamber of Deputies, 28.4.1845.

[57] *OE. C.* IV, 248. *L'Ancien Régime.*

[58] *OE. C.* I, 67.

[59] *OE. C.* III, 546. *De la Démocratie en Amérique.*

[60] '*la dernière trace des rangs et des distinctions héréditaires est détruite*'. *OE. C.* I, 81. *De la Démocratie en Amérique.*

[61] *OE. C.* VIII, 327.

[62] *OE. C.* VIII, 327ff.

[63] *OE. C.* I, 7. *De la Démocratie en Amérique.*

[64] '*Pense-t-on qu'après avoir détruit la féodalité et vaincu les rois, la démocratie reculera devant les bourgeois et les riches? S'arrêtera-t-elle maintenant qu'elle est devenue si forte et ses adversaires si faibles?*' Ibid., p. 8.

[65] *l'état social que leur impose la Providence.* Ibid., p. 7.

# CHAPTER III
## Doubt

With some thinkers, enthusiasm for an ideal tends to melt away as they realise how remote are the chances of its fruition. With others, affection becomes stronger as the possibility of its realisation diminishes. The latter say that it is not the defects of the ideal but the perversity of the men for whom it is designed which prevents its realisation. The curious paradox that confronts the student of human ideals is that the men who have excited the attention of mankind with their vision of good societies are generally very pessimistic about human nature. Indeed, the source of their inspiration is often disgust with the activities of the normal human being. And when the normal man's response to their ideals is indifference or opposition, the idealist uses this behaviour as evidence of his contention that human nature is the stumbling-block in the way of the good society. If he is strong-minded, he may devote his energies to the conversion of mankind; if he is weak, he will withdraw from human society, and satisfy his craving for the ideal by contemplating the perfect life in some future world. From 1835–48, Tocqueville belonged to the former category, believing that to realise his ideal, he must convert men from the values and behaviour which disposed them to accept the contrary to his ideal. As we shall see, the experiences of 1848–51 were so distressing that he spent the last eight years of his life resisting the temptation to accept the thesis of the pessimists that men were eternally incapable of the good life.

But despair is not the prevailing state of his mind in the era of the bourgeois monarchy. Despair seeps through when the anxieties of those days are all too vividly fulfilled in the dictatorship of Louis Napoleon. The most persistent of these is the question: how will men use the liberties necessary for the pursuit of the ideal of liberty? He analyses the dangerous situation with masterly penetration, displays to the full the genius of the 'cool head'. But when it comes to suggesting a remedy, his personal sensibilities make him shrink before a radical solution.

This hesitation is most marked in his discussion of the liberties. The assumption in establishing freedom of the press, liberty of association and political liberty is that they will be used to do what is good and just. But will they? The strongest motive in the lives of his contemporaries is the pursuit of material well-being; values, political institutions and social systems are judged by the degree to which they assist the pursuit of this ideal. Any one of these liberties may aggravate political disturbances which affect material prosperity.

'*Emeutes*' [disturbances] destroy social peace. The fear of anarchy keeps the people in nervous suspense—a suspense from which they obtain relief by supporting any government which can guarantee public order even if that government withdraws the liberties essential for the pursuit of his ideal. A nation which demands from its government only the maintenance of order is already enslaved in its heart. The man or party to carry out the *coup de grâce* will soon appear. And the men who received their liberties for the purpose of pursuing the ideal of liberty will use their pens to propagate opinions favourable to this government, their clubs to influence others, and their votes to elect them to office.[1] One other example of this potential misuse of the liberties before we notice their effects. Men who concentrate on the accumulation of wealth sever nearly all relations with other human beings; they suffer from what he calls spiritual loneliness.[2] In their isolation they look for a support to bear their burdens, share their anxieties. Men with such spiritual complaints are attracted to the 'big man'—'*le soutien unique et nécessaire*' [their sole and indispensable support]. Here too is a motive for using the liberties to promote their own well-being by destroying liberty.

This anxiety as to the use of the liberties becomes even more intelligible when we read his imaginary sketch of the type of life permitted in a society which had used its liberties to establish such a régime. There would be an immense population of men, all equal and similar to each other, incessantly engaged in obtaining the petty and vulgar pleasures which would be all they demanded of life. Each man would live for himself and his narrow circle of intimates, and be an indifferent stranger to the rest of humanity. Over these individuals the State would watch—a vast, intricate administration which provided for every need and controlled every action of the individual; benevolent, provided its universal authority were not questioned; relieving him of all major decisions, indeed, making it almost unnecessary for him to think—or live. Thus individual liberty would be exercised ever less frequently and less effectively until it atrophied altogether.[3]

In such a society, the activities which Tocqueville cultivated would wither away. Men might be happy, but not great. Great actions and manly virtues would not be performed by men whose minds were fixed '*irrévocablement dans l'enfance*' [irrevocably in childhood]. On the other hand, the wants which he despised would be freely indulged—'*petits et vulgaires plaisirs*' [petty and vulgar pleasures]. How could men pursue liberty when they were deprived of the minimum prerequisites—the pleasure of thinking, speaking and writing without compulsion?

Tocqueville was not impressed by the arguments with which some of his contemporaries assured themselves that such a despotism could not happen in the 19th century—the century of progress, of hope and enlightenment. What was to prevent it? The prestige formerly enjoyed by the legitimate rulers of society had been destroyed by the French Revolution. The checks and restraints upon the powers of a despot over his subjects had been swept away in the avalanche at the end of the 18th century. Before the Revolution, the king was loved and respected as the '*père de l'Etat*' [father of the nation]: after it, he became a '*maître*' [master] for whom the people felt contempt if he was weak, and hatred if he was strong.[4]

Even if the pre-revolutionary king exceeded the powers conferred on him by the law, his subjects could appeal to a higher authority—the moral law as interpreted by the Church. But the attacks on the Church at the end of the 18th century had undermined the power which it formerly exercised over the minds of men. And if there was no moral law accepted by all men, who could say where the powers of a despot ended, who could condemn his behaviour by an appeal to a law or a principle acceptable to all men? So Tocqueville's retort to the optimists is: where is the creed to restrain the desire for a despot? And so long as he is engaged in an analysis of the problem we are forced to admire the skill with which it is presented, the insight which enabled him to prophesy accurately the main features of the Fascist régimes of the 20th century, and the zeal with which he propagated this unpopular opinion. After all, a man who prophesies a regression when others are eagerly anticipating the millennium needs the courage of his convictions.[h] But it is when the analysis ceases and the solution is offered that approval ceases. The reader's mind holds back just when Tocqueville begins to warm to his theme.

The answer to the desire for material well-being is perhaps the best example of the operations of his mind. We do not question the accuracy of his observation: for the bourgeois Gold was God,[5] or, as Balzac conceived it, usury was the compass by which all classes directed their lives.[6] What we do question is the validity of his explanation—that this is one of the effects of equality. Now as Tocqueville believed that love of equality was one of the permanent qualities in human nature (see above), he naturally inferred that pursuit of wealth and its attendant characteristics—the desire to 'get on' and jealousy of superior qualities—were also permanent motives of human conduct. True, wherever he had observed equality, there also were the other qualities—in America and in England. But it was not even true that the one was the cause of the other. Even in his time there were egalitarian societies without these features. In French Canada there was equality of conditions but not that go-ahead spirit, that restless, impatient eagerness for improvement of circumstances,

---

[h]  On p. 53 of the copy text, Clark inserts a marginal note: 'Incidentally this idea is developed much more fiercely by Ivan Karamazov in his fantasy on the Grand Inquisitor' F. Dostoevsky [*The Brothers Karamazov*].

that absence of classes and class spirit, that jealousy of superior attainments, which Tocqueville attributed to equality in the United States of America.[7] Indeed, the very contrary qualities prevailed in that country.

The fact was that both his cause, equality, and his effect, pursuit of wealth, were themselves the effect of a cause which Tocqueville almost completely ignored—the rise of modern industry, and the values of the class directing this development.[8] And because he confounds both cause and effect, he infers that these desires must be sublimated by an appeal to some other motive in man. So instead of the empirical proposition that this behaviour was the effect of economic causes, his mind was haunted by the awful spectre that there was something permanently vicious and loathsome in man which could be restrained only by a discipline imposed by some external authority. To remove the obstacles between his ideal and its realisation, the idealist turns for support not to man, but to the heavenly powers.

There is no logical objection to the conclusion of his argument if its assumptions—love of equality and material well-being as permanent qualities in human nature—are conceded. Religion inspires the contrary 'instincts' in man. Every religion directs man's desires to an object higher than mere worldly possessions, and raises his soul to regions superior to those of the senses. The men who have assented to these truths have understood the Divine Will. What is more, they will be able to perceive the truth that individual material interests must be sacrificed for the sake of a 'higher order'.[9] Later we shall discuss the consequences of using religion as the instrument by which these desires can be sublimated.

Here let us notice this: if religion is the effective antidote to the desires of men, it must also be the best guarantee for the proper use of the liberties. This was not a truth arrived at by logical argument, but a deduction from his observations in America. There men did not behave in an undesirable way, nor did they hold opinions inimical to the survival of liberty. And why? The law permitted them to think and act as they pleased, but their religious beliefs forbade them 'to conceive all and to dare all'.[10] If religious beliefs ensured the proper use of the liberties in America, surely the same satisfactory results would be obtained in Europe if the same method were used. At least Tocqueville could see no other answer to the problem of the liberties: men are not free without them, but with them they may choose to make themselves permanently unfree. The discussion of each one of the liberties leads to the same question: how to ensure their proper use?

First: liberty of the press. The definition entails no restrictions upon the liberty of the citizen to express in speech or writing any opinions which he wishes to communicate to his fellow-men. Yet, as Tocqueville realised, men may use this liberty to express opinions hostile to liberty, and they may persuade others to act on these opinions. The example we have used already—the desire for social peace to ensure material well-being—will provide an illustration of this dilemma. Men were, he believed, strongly attached to material satisfactions because they were more obvious and easier to achieve than the spiritual. As a result they were more likely to be persuaded by the opinions which flattered and appealed to these passions than by the opinions which appealed to their 'higher natures'. Unless restrictions were imposed on the liberty of the press, what could prevent the perversion (from his point of view) of their minds by these insidiously attractive opinions?

But any restriction imposed by the law was incompatible with liberty. Besides, by what criterion were they to censor one opinion and permit publication of another? He liked to think that there was an intermediate position between the extremes of complete liberty and absolute restrictions—a position which would suppress dangerous opinions, but provide some scope for the exercise of the liberty.[11] The 'cool head' which was impressed with the importance of unrestricted liberty of the press, evidently prevailed over his personal fear of the consequences. And so the discussion of the problem ends with suggestions for a restraint which would be not legal but moral: religion is introduced as the effective restraint. Men with religious beliefs do not entertain dangerous or insidious opinions. Why impose restrictions by law, and diminish the liberty of the citizen, when religion itself ensures that men will use this liberty properly?

The interesting point is that the solution to the dilemma removes the necessity to answer the empirical question: what are the sources of the diversity of opinions? If Tocqueville had posed this question, he might have arrived at the simple conclusion that men who live differently will think differently. From this he might have concluded the inquiry on a more empirical note: that it was important to establish the social conditions favourable to his values. But the solution which he puts forward minimises the importance of social conditions; no matter what thoughts are stimulated by the conditions under which men live, religious beliefs ensure that the opinions they express will be correct. The Indian peasant eking out his filthy existence on a miserable pittance—in some cases only a penny a day—will not be influenced by revolutionary propaganda if his religious faith stands the strain of this degrading environment. Perhaps the example is an extreme one. But the use of religion to ensure correct opinions is redolent of notions of resignation to material hardship. We may admire the logical precision with which the argument is conducted, but we would do well to notice the conditions which may exist at the same time, of which the argument, while not stating positive approval, makes no criticism. It is pleasing to know that no one will be persuaded by speech or writing to strike another person, but it is shocking to know that inaction implies resignation to material conditions which would revolt even the members of the brute creation.

The discussion of liberty of association begins with the same problem: the dangers of unrestricted liberty. A society may be divided on fundamental questions. In such a contingency a minority party may not be prepared to accept the decisions of the majority. Will this party limit its activities to talking and writing? How long will it accept the metaphysical consideration that the aim of associations is to direct opinions and not to constrain them, to offer counsel but not to make the law by force?[12] It would be crass stupidity to grant unrestricted liberty of association when certain associations intended to use this liberty to destroy liberty. How can restrictions be justified? The answer is oddly in contrast to the solution of the analogous dilemma raised by the liberty of the press: these associations must be suppressed, not because they infringe the moral law, but because they endanger the safety of the state.[13] It is not difficult to account for this difference in opinion. Liberty of association did not affect him personally, as did the liberty of speech and writing. Restriction is repugnant to the 'cool head' but not to the 'burning passions'. During his own life he never became a member of a political party; nor, as far as we know, was he a member of any of the social or political clubs in Paris. Why should a man who experienced such painful sensations in associating with any but the very few feel strongly in favour of unrestricted liberty of association?

And if he was emotionally disinterested, he was all the more willing to be persuaded by the arguments for restriction. There were at least two parties in France at that time—the Carlists and the Bonapartists—who threatened to overthrow the existing régime by force, and Tocqueville prepared and wrote the first two volumes of *De la Démocratie en Amérique* at the same time as the two abortive 'disturbances' of the thirties—the Carlist rising in Brittany and Louis Napoleon's fiasco which ended at Ham. 'Disturbances' distressed him even more than the behaviour of the bourgeois. His wife and intimate friends alone knew the agonies he had experienced in Paris in July 1830.[i] Later on we shall see how his judgement was affected by the June days in 1848.

The curious thing is that where he is emotionally disposed to accept restriction, neither the rationalisation of these desires nor their justification is secured by an appeal to a more compelling principle than expediency. Granted his values, it may be expedient to dissolve the Carlists and the Bonapartists, but the same argument can be used against the associations he approves of. In 1851 the Bonapartists dissolved the liberal associations because they endangered the safety of the state. Still, in 1835 this was a remote possibility, so Tocqueville assumes that all <u>right-thinking</u> men will approve of the restrictions he advocates.

The interesting point is that when the discussion is brought to a conclusion without resorting to metaphysical support, he perceives

---

[i] On p. 59 of the copy text, Clark inserts a marginal note: 'There is a letter in the archives at Tocqueville written to Marie Mottley in which he expresses his reactions to the street fighting in 1830'.

that the need for a principle to justify restriction will be less strongly felt in proportion to the similarity of opinions expressed in a society. Where this similarity exists, 'in a country like the United States, where opinions differ only very slightly, virtually unrestricted freedom of association may in effect prevail'.[14] But the observation does not excite him. The emotional arguments for restriction are so strong that even the liberty of the subject must be curtailed.[j] Nor is there more than a bleat of regret: men would still be free. Perhaps being free means associating to promote the principles he approves of!

The same dilemma is posed by the methods used to elect a government. The ideal entails no restrictions on the right to vote except age and residence, but the effects of universal franchise may be disastrous to the very ideal it is designed to serve. The vote may aggravate the antagonism between rich and poor; indeed the poor may use the vote to legalise the expropriation of the rich, and, as the rich are in a minority in society, they will be compelled to resort to violence to offset the designs of the poor. There is a simple and obvious solution to this problem: give the poor a vested interest in the rights of property, because 'in proportion as the people acquire property . . . they have less need of the money of the wealthy'.[15] Universal franchise did not aggravate class relations in America, because there was no property-less class in that country.

But even if this antagonism could be minimised by adjustment of income levels, his crucial doubts on the effects of universal franchise remained unanswered: will the people select the best men, and what protection has a minority against the will of the majority? Affection for equality entails not only disapproval of economic inequality, but a jealousy of all superior attainments; any mark of superiority is intolerable to men infected with its spirit. Men whose actions are determined by these emotions will use their votes to exclude any distinguished candidate, and to elect the mediocrities. What was even more alarming was the tendency for men of distinc-

---

[j]  On p. 60 of the copy text, Clark inserts a marginal note: 'Does this contradict early reference to lib. [liberty] of assoc. [association]?'

tion to become more and more rare in a democratic society.* In an aristocratic society there was a steady stream of men with the right qualities—'mighty and enlightened men'—but democratic societies behaved as if governed by a modified Gresham's law. The mediocre drove out the talented; 'hence they do not produce individuals of this calibre'. But even if the judgement of the masses was not distorted by their innate jealousy of the talented, they lacked both the mental equipment and the knowledge with which to choose 'those men best able to govern'. [16] Why not educate the masses? This was the solution of the Americans—'education, they said, is the only guarantee we have against the aberrations of the masses'.[17] But education could not change habits of thought. What was required was a number of men holding *convictions réfléchies* [well-considered convictions]. But only the very few achieved this position; the majority of men were attached inseparably to their own interests.

The point was—though he never declared it to himself—that his conception of man, if true, made his ideal chimerical. Liberty, by his conception, entailed universal franchise: but the ideal assumed a society of *'gens supérieurs'* [superior individuals], not a majority of *'gens médiocres'* [mediocre individuals]; men with high standards, not content with *'un mitoyen médiocre'* [a middling average]. Once again the belief in innate qualities is a stumbling-block to the realisation of his ideal. The curious thing is that the depressing conclusion is almost lost to sight in the grandiloquent language in which the problem is discussed. The subtle flattery of the reader, the memorable phrases used to impress the problem on his mind, and then the stirring reference to the importance of the problem for the future of mankind: it is as though the author and the reader were the sole arbiters of human destiny—so much so that the critical faculty is silenced until the spell is over. Here is a brief example of his skill in eliciting the sympathies of his audience: it comes from a letter to

---

* He noticed this first during the American journey: 'Why, when civilisation spreads, do the outstanding men grow fewer? Why, when there are no longer any lower classes, are there no superior classes? Why, when the knowledge of government reaches the masses, are great geniuses missing from the direction of society?' (Quoted in G. W. Pierson: *Tocqueville and Beaumont in America*, p. 510).

John Stuart Mill and was written shortly after the completion of *De la Démocratie en Amérique*: 'For the supporters of democracy, it is not so much a matter of seeing to it that the people actually govern, as of ensuring that they elect the men best able to govern and of giving the people sufficient authority over their representatives to direct the general conduct of government but not the details of legislation or the method of implementation. This is the problem. I am completely convinced that the fate of the modern nation states depends on its solution. But how few people even realise this! And how few draw attention to it!'[18] How few! The eternal lament at the ignorance and the indifference of the masses. We may indeed wonder that the ignorant masses should be allowed to direct general policy—but we cannot fail to detect the omission of a solution to the problem of the unenlightened electorate. If the fate of the modern world depended on the election of men with the right qualities, it was clearly his duty to consider the cognate problems—the selection and education of these men. But Tocqueville was content with the reflection. His mind runs on to the pious hope that in small units men would be able to recognise the men with superior talents and would choose them as their representatives. His mind can find no arguments with which to nourish this hope.

If the discussion on the election of 'superior individuals' peters out because his faith in the common man is too weak, the discussion of safeguards against the tyranny of the majority brings us back to the familiar dilemma of the liberties. The majority may vote for one policy and the minority for another. Must the minority accept the decisions of the majority? Tocqueville says no: the people have not the right to do everything—that was an immoral and detestable doctrine—but only the right to do 'that which is just'.[19] The law of justice was a higher authority than the sovereignty of the people. Who is the interpreter of this law of justice and how does it operate? In one passage Tocqueville seems to suggest that the 'superior individuals' are the interpreters of this law. The opinions of the people, when they are reasonable and correct, ought to govern the conduct of those in charge of affairs—that is the democratic principle.

But democratic principles do not require that they should follow popular passions, nor the momentary impulses of the mob when under the influence of men who deliberately flatter their prejudices in order to induce them to betray their true interests. Generally the people want the public good, but they are often deceived in their search for it. When the true interests of the people are contrary to its desires, then it is the duty of all those whom it has elected to take care of its interests to fight the error so as to give the people time to reconsider the situation and debate the question in a calmer mood. There have been occasions when the people, who have been saved in this way from the fatal consequences of their own errors, have raised monuments to those men who have had the courage to expose themselves to popular odium in order to serve the people.[20] Public monuments as evidence of observance of the law of justice add an almost comic note to a very unconvincing argument. The motives of the 'superior individuals' may be just as false as the motives of the people, while their appeal to the law of justice to justify opposition to the majority reads more like an effective device to silence the demands of the working classes than an impartial defence of the principles of justice. Besides, if this 'law of justice' is no more than a rationalisation of the desires (interests) of the upper classes, the anger of the lower classes will be directed not only against the class frustrating its demands, but against the creed used to justify that resistance. Religion will be discredited. The creed which prevents men from 'conceiving and daring all' will be derided and cursed by the very men whose passions it was designed to subdue. In this case moral anarchy would result. Moral anarchy—the very words should be sufficient to make Tocqueville wary of killing the goose (religion) which lays the golden egg: the proper use of the liberties.

Yet if a man has suffered an injustice at the hands of the majority in a democratic society, how can he obtain redress without appealing to some external authority? He may appeal to public opinion. There he will find the majority whose decision he opposes. The legislature? But the legislature is the voice of public opinion. The executive? It too is nominated by the majority and serves it obediently. The army? It is the majority under arms. A jury, or a law court? Again he will find the majority, their decisions endowed with the force of law. Against a majority endowed with such power, the opinions or behaviour of an individual or a minority party are powerless. Nor is injustice to individuals or minority parties the sole evil of rule by the majority.[21] Unless there is an external authority, the sole sanction for an action is that it is done with the consent of the majority. The greatest crimes may be justified by this doctrine. Worse, the most extreme form of servitude, unrestricted personal despotism, may be justified as a faithful fulfilment of the wishes of the majority: 'It might be possible to induce [them] to concede to him these unlimited powers when he seemed to represent the national sovereignty. In this way Napoleon was ultimately able to claim, without greatly offending public opinion, that he had the right to take command of everything because he alone spoke in the name of the people'.[22]

Tocqueville is not comforted by the reflection that truth will ultimately prevail. Under a Napoleon the suppression of the liberty of the press is also justified as the will of the majority. But even in societies where free speech and writing are tolerated the majority will stubbornly maintain its faith in its original opinion: nothing is more difficult than to eradicate an idea once it has established itself firmly in the minds of the people. Moreover any constitutional machinery devised as a corrective to the tyranny of the majority errs in one of two directions: it either transfers power from the majority to a minority—generally the upper classes—or it still permits the majority to rule despite the checks and balances devised to restrain its powers. Tocqueville's own proposals suffer from both these faults. His ideal legislature would represent the majority, but not be the willing instrument of its passions—an attractive plan because no one who has studied the behaviour of men when enslaved to their passions would object to proposals to eliminate this influence. But the method—double election—would mean that the voting power of the minority, the 'superior individuals', would be greater than that of the majority.[23] The passions are the pretext for disenfranchising undesirable electors. Every deviation from the simple principle— one vote, one value—is designed to transfer power from the majority to the minority. The other two institutions—the executive and the judiciary—were to be independent both of the legislature and each other.

This idea of separation of powers was borrowed directly from Montesquieu. (*De l'Esprit des Lois* was one of the very few books on political philosophy which Tocqueville studied carefully.) But both Montesquieu and Tocqueville overlooked the simple fact that political institutions are the servants of the men who create them. They missed the point that even in England, where there appeared to be separation of powers, all three institutions—legislature, executive and judiciary—were the medium by which the governing class exercised its power, some would say tyranny! Even if there is a separation of powers, the same social class may control all three institutions. The tyranny against which he was protesting would be less obvious, but just as effective: the governing class will have a vested interest in suppressing the opinions and behaviour which threaten their tenure of power. All attempts to curb the power of the majority either vitiate the democratic principle of equality, or fail to achieve their purpose. The man who refuses to accept the decisions of the majority may find support for his disapproval in the 'law of justice', but no hope of a practical remedy. For that he must strive to equate the decisions of the majority with the principles of that law. To believe in such a possibility one must have faith in human progress and Tocqueville is not responsive to such optimism. The men he had observed were inseparably attached to their material interests. Conversion was impossible: discipline was the one corrective to the decisions of such a majority. Religion is the big stick with which to subdue the bourgeois and the working man. All the constitutional safeguards against abuse of these powers are as chaff before the wind; religion, on the other hand, guarantees that the wind will not even rise.

His interest in the effects of political liberty is not confined to the quest for a corrective to the actions of the majority. He was uneasy not only because they might use the liberties badly, but also because they might not want to use them at all. The obligation to participate in the administration of the commune, province or nation is an irritating distraction to men whose primary interest is in their own welfare. Nor is it easy for them to perceive the effect of their own actions if they do fulfil their political duties. It is this conviction of the ineffectiveness of his own actions which strengthens a citizen's desire to remain aloof from all political activities. Men who prefer indifference to responsibility welcome any opportunity to abandon their political duties to officials. Nor do they expect these officials to observe any other principles than efficiency and stability. Tocqueville was alarmed by this tendency because its final form, administrative centralisation, excluded political liberty.[24] What he noticed was that governments were either assuming more and more power without protest, or might receive an unqualified mandate from the people to abolish all institutions—local councils, parliaments, etc.—which required the exercise of political liberty.

This insistence on the importance of participation in the affairs of a country for the survival of liberty is perhaps Tocqueville's most important contribution to the political thought of his time. The societies which permitted the abolition of their political liberties have suffered a corresponding withdrawal of liberty, while those who vigorously maintained them have preserved intact at least the conditions prescribed for the pursuit of liberty. The French bourgeois who lived for the Bourse, and allowed M. le Préfet to administer the affairs of his commune or *département* has had two régimes which curtailed or removed the liberties—Napoleon III and Vichy. The German bourgeois who was eliminated from the political life of his community by the feudal notion that politics is the preserve of princes and nobles, or who comforted himself with the assurance that *akademische Freiheit* [academic freedom] is more important than freedom to act, has had only one dose of political liberty [under the democratic Weimar Republic, 1919–33]. This experience left such an unpleasant taste in his mouth that he was prepared to endure the most complete destruction of his liberties rather than continue with the experiment. England, the mother, and America, the child of political liberty, have retained their liberties. Indeed, in 1852 England was so strongly attached to her liberties that she had become 'the grand jury of mankind in the cause of freedom'.[25]

Here was a crucial problem for a believer in liberty: indifference, not a desire to participate, is the natural attitude to political duties. The effect of this indifference is fatal to liberty. The solution is to provide an antidote to the symptom, indifference. Men are all too easily inclined to think of nothing but their private interests, to consider themselves only and thus to sink into the narrow precincts of self, in which all interest in public affairs is completely extinguished.[26] Religion inspires the sentiments to combat these insidious values. Christianity exhorts us to take interest in the affairs of others, to do good to our fellow human beings—'a truly magnificent concept'.[27] But this moral obligation is but a tender plant in a wilderness of poisonous weeds. Without careful cultivation it may wither away.

Curiously enough, the impulse to participate in public affairs for the common good is strengthened by the exercise of the very rights which the baser self encourages men to ignore. 'Freedom alone can effectually counteract in communities of this kind the vices which are natural to them and restrain them on the declivity down which they glide. For freedom alone can withdraw the members of such a community from the isolation in which the very dependence on their conditions places them by compelling them to act together. Freedom alone can warm and unite them day by day through the necessity for mutual agreement, for mutual persuasion, and mutual goodwill in the transaction of their common affairs . . .'[28] Notice the change in values which occurs: when not using this liberty they believe that indifference to the affairs of others is the *summum bonum* [the highest good]; when exercising it they find participation to be a greater good than indifference. Liberty introduces them to a 'higher life'; the intolerable burden becomes a joy.[29]

But perhaps this lyrical language is more a pleasing fantasy of what men might experience if they fulfilled their duties than a prophecy of what would in fact occur. The moral obligation sublimates but does not destroy the <u>innate</u> selfishness. It is this which explains the attraction of centralisation, of despotism—the antithesis of his ideal. And so long as his mind is convinced that men have this 'instinct' or 'natural tendency to centralise power'[30] the conditions for the pursuit of liberty must be artificial and precarious; the innate desires of man may at any time burst through the dykes containing them.

This judgement does not rest upon an inadequate knowledge of past events. In both *L'Etat de la France avant et depuis 1789* and *L'Ancien Régime et la Révolution* he sketched the evolution of administrative centralisation. But history is used, not to prove that institutions change in response to human needs, but as proof for the 'instinct' and the 'natural tendency'. Nowhere does he even hint that administrative centralisation, with its ubiquitous organs of standing army, police, bureaucracy, clergy and judicature, was designed primarily to serve the needs of the bourgeoisie as a mighty weapon in its struggle against feudalism; that with their final victory over the old society in 1830, these powers were increased to protect the economic interests of the bourgeoisie and to repress the classes which challenged their tenure of power.[31] And perhaps if he had perceived that this class antagonism never developed into civil war simply because of those very state powers which made him apprehensive for the future of liberty, he might have paid more attention to the cause of this antagonism.

But the vision of a society in which the main cause of centralisation is removed is denied him by the conviction that the symptoms he deplores are evidence of the innate qualities in man. And so long as he held to this position he was perforce pessimistic about the results of human endeavour; he advised his friends not to expect too much from man. This lack of faith in man caused him to look for his redeemer outside human society; even man's apparent attraction to administrative centralisation is to be sublimated by 'higher discipline'. The man who wrote such a lugubrious account of a society deprived of its liberties, and had such a splendid vision of a free society, was not a profound believer in the human material for whom his ideal was designed. Perhaps ideals are illusions in which the refined find compensation for the unpleasant experiences in this world; the visions of harmony distract their mind from the depressing conclusions which an objective survey of the facts might force them to draw. At least with Tocqueville any confidence in the application of his ideal is always deflated by doubts on the goodness of man. The significant thing is that these doubts spring from an unwillingness to perceive that the material interests of man—which he despises—are variable. It is the failure to examine closely the causes of these changes which produces the stumbling-block in all his problems.

The discussion of the type of society favourable to the pursuit of his ideal ends on a similar note: the good society is the product of men of good-will. It begins with the declaration of a principle: economic equality is the most favourable social setting for the pursuit of liberty. 'I think that it would be impossible to present men with a great alternative of strength and weakness, to allow them to enjoy extreme equality in one respect and to endure extreme inequality in other respects—without them soon either aspiring to be strong, or becoming weak in all respects'.[32] Inequality is a hindrance to that state of mind essential for the proper use of the liberties: it excites the passions of both rich and poor. It may seem odd to some that this timid, cautious observer of human events should have assented to such a daring principle, especially as opinion at that time was so hostile to economic equality, while its devotees were branded as atheists or corrupters of youth. But then who could object to the polite phrases of M. de Tocqueville? Did he not ask men to believe in equality, not so that they might fill their stomachs but to fill their souls? Besides, in *De la Démocratie en Amérique* excessive economic inequality and the attendant social problems are only mentioned as a remote possibility. Indeed, the disinterested manner in which he discussed the subject allowed his mind to work uninhibited by the emotions.

The result was a brilliant and prophetic sketch of the evolution of capitalist society. The theme was that if the capitalists were permitted to build an economic system to serve their needs there would be extreme economic inequality—'Industry might, in its turn, lead men back towards aristocracy'.[33] The aim of the capitalist was to increase his profits, and the rate of profit depended on his ability to produce a large volume of goods at a low cost. The quantity could be increased by specialisation of labour.[34] At the same time the capitalist would reduce his costs by paying his workmen the lowest possible wage. These developments would place working men in an awkward dilemma: poverty would cause a demand for an improvement in their conditions, but specialisation deprives them of the means by which to rise from the bottom rung of the economic ladder—'an industrial theory ties him to one trade, and often to one locality, which he cannot leave . . . This theory has assigned him a certain position in society from which he cannot extricate himself'.[35]

So much for the operation of economic laws. But working men did not accept the arguments for subordination which had governed the relations between '*seigneur*' [master] and '*laquais*' [servant] under the *ancien régime*. The 'servant' obeyed the 'master' first because he inherited the habit of obedience; from infancy the notion of subservience and servility was inculcated into his mind. Habit was reinforced by the benefits received from the 'master'—benefits which they believed depended on their tacit acceptance of a subordinate position. In an industrial society, working men enjoyed no benefits except a bare subsistence from obeying the behests of their masters. Finally, the 'servant' accepted subordination as part of the will of Providence. Did not the Church teach that it was sinful to rebel against their masters? In industrial society the Church continued its teaching, but the hearts of the workers had been hardened against its doctrines by the conviction that the Church had a vested interest in the survival of the economic slavery against which they were protesting.[36]

Even here his personal sympathies are with the relationship between the 'master' and the 'servant'. He lingers fondly over the habits of their society, and ignores the distasteful side—the arrogance of the 'master' and the servility of the 'servant'. But if sentiment impels him to write of their way of life with warmth and affection, reflection suggests that the arguments for subordination have lost their force—'obedience is losing its moral force in the eyes of the obedient . . . in their eyes it is neither sacred nor just'.[37] Working men will not endure misery while their masters enjoy the wealth created by their labour. The soil is trembling again in Europe. A revolutionary wind is in the air. The new economic conditions will create new political and social issues—'There can scarcely be any doubt that soon the party struggle will be between those who have and those who have not . . . and the main issues in politics will revolve round the extent to which the rights of property owners should be modified.'[38]

It is an acute and penetrating analysis of the evolution of capitalist society. His insistence on the disharmony of interests between masters and men in a capitalist democracy, and their probable issue in revolution, suggests analogies with Marx.[39] But the analogy ends with his diagnosis. For the solution Tocqueville is obliged to observe the standards dictated by his ideal. It is not purely a question of the necessity for equality but of the reasons adduced to establish the necessity and the methods by which it is introduced. The right of everyone to an equal share in the products of industry is suspect as the doctrine of the materialists. Nor must there be compulsion, for compulsion may produce equality, but at the expense of liberty. In the 1830s the solution suggested is too indefinite to gauge the trend of his ideas: he said then that the poverty of the working man should receive the special attention of the legislator.[40]

Nor does the imminence of revolution produce any clearer statement of the policy required to achieve equality. This time the legislator is exhorted to provide for the welfare of the workers. But there is a difference between the recommendations of the thirties and the forties—a difference in emotional tension. In 1848, on the eve of the February Revolution, he was prepared to get down on his knees before the Chamber, if they would be favourably impressed by this gesture—*tant je crois le danger réel et sérieux* [so real and serious do I believe the danger to be]. In his excitement he reveals the methods by which he hoped to achieve equality. There was no need to change the laws, for they do not in themselves decide the fate of nations. There was no need to change the personnel of the government. What must be changed was the *esprit* [spirit] of the men in the governing class, because it was this 'spirit' which was leading them to the abyss.[41]

A change of heart must precede the adjustment of income levels. For then the rich would <u>voluntarily</u> share their wealth with the poor; harmony of interests would be established not by compulsion, the threat of the poor to expropriate the rich, but by an agreement to share their material resources. The poor shall embrace their oppressors—the lion shall lie down with the unicorn—these are the visions excited by the contemplation of men who have experienced this change of heart. Is this sentimental nonsense, or are there good reasons for believing in this life of regenerated men? Tocqueville relies on religion to prepare men's hearts for economic equality. It is the 'higher discipline' which encouraged him to believe in his ideal even though the desires and interests of men conflicted with it.

The usual criticism of this position is to refuse to accept the religious beliefs because there is no demonstration of their truth. But even if they are not true it may still be desirable to have an authority which restrains the actions of men. And Tocqueville's position is not: 'I believe in God, and therefore I believe in discipline imposed on men'; but rather, 'I notice the consequences of absence of restraint on human actions and disapprove: I believe that these consequences would not occur if man accepted the "higher discipline"'. In the French Revolution religious laws were destroyed at the same time as the political laws—'the human mind completely lost its bearings'. Man no longer knew what was right and what was wrong. Men of a new type appeared, who 'carried audacity to the point of madness', 'who could not be surprised by anything new or deterred by any scruple, and who never hesitated to execute any scheme whatsoever'.[42] Tocqueville's position is that if religious beliefs are revived, they will restrain this behaviour—the undesirable consequences of scepticism will disappear.

But if we assume such a revival, what ethical consequences are entailed? A bewildering and conflicting variety of human behaviour acquires a very reassuring justification. In the south of the United States of America, for example, religious beliefs provided a justification for slavery, while in the north they provided the moral arguments for the crusade against that institution. In France the institution interpreting religious beliefs—the Catholic Church—was openly hostile to the very ideal he was recommending: liberty. Not only the workers, but the free-thinkers, all the sincere men of every institution and society who wanted liberty, were critical of the Church.[43]

And yet Tocqueville insisted that without religious beliefs liberty could not survive: 'If liberty breaks away finally and completely from religious belief, it will always lack that element of . . . stability, tranquillity, vitality, which alone makes it great and fruitful'.[44] If the Church is opposed to liberty and the supporters of liberty to the

Church, Tocqueville must convert the Church to liberty and the liberals to the Church. The objection we make to this proposal is not the hopelessness of the task—though the experience of F. R. Lamennais and the Catholic Liberals does suggest that it was almost a superhuman task—but the confusion which this modification of religious beliefs placed him in.

We are told that religious beliefs are a restraint upon the actions of men, an assurance that men will use their liberties to do what is good and just. To be universally effective these religious beliefs must be incorporated in a church or other religious institution which must claim to be infallible. The religious institution in France in Tocqueville's day was of course the Catholic Church. He was unable to accept the body of Catholic doctrine as infallible, except where it coincided with his own views, and considered all the other doctrines to be in need of revision. In other words, to him religion was mainly a support for his own personal views on the good society. There was nothing to prevent any other man with political ambitions or ideals from evolving another religion which would support an entirely different view of society and attempting to set it up as the arbiter of public morals. In fact, this was at that moment being done by other political thinkers, such as de Bonald, who stated the case for an authoritarian government justified by religion in his work: *Les vrais Principes opposés aux erreurs du 19e siècle.*

A state religion as a restraint on men's conduct created two difficulties. To begin with, men were unwilling to submit to a religion which set out deliberately to restrain some of their strongest desires. And even if they were prepared to accept such a state religion, it would seem almost impossible to achieve agreement on its doctrines. Yet without such a discipline Tocqueville can see no hope for the proper use of the liberties. Nor can he anticipate the eradication of the qualities in human nature—affection for the material satisfactions, envy of superior attainments—which hinder the pursuit of his ideal.

If religion fails in its task of directing human behaviour along the right channels, the liberties can be introduced in two other ways: either, as in England or Soviet Russia, on condition that they are not used to incite men to overthrow the existing régime—which is a restriction of liberty; or, as in France and in Germany under the Weimar Republic, without restrictions—which led to anarchy and the conviction that order was a greater good than liberty. True: both these latter examples seem to uphold Tocqueville's dictum that where men do not accept restraint upon their actions, liberty will not endure. But the difficulty is to find a restraint which is acceptable to all men, and at the same time effective. His restraint—religious beliefs—only aggravates the conflict of interests in society. What is more serious: the men who use this authority often tend to do so to secure their own interests, which are favoured by the existing order. A religious idealist is often the bitterest opponent of those men who attempt to create a better society for all men in this world.

## Endnotes

1. *OE. C.* III, 228. *De la Démocratie en Amérique.*
2. Ibid., III, 482.
3. Ibid., III, 519.
4. Ibid., II, 254.
5. H. Heine: *Sämmtliche Werke* IX, p. 257.
6. H. Balzac: *Les Employés*, p. 64.
7. J. S. Mill: *Dissertations and Discussions* II, p. 63.
8. Ibid.
9. *OE.C.* III, 205. *De la Démocratie en Amérique.*
10. '*de tout concevoir et de tout oser*'. Ibid., II, 217.
11. Ibid., II, 16–20.
12. Ibid., II, 34.
13. Ibid., II, 35.
14. '*dans un pays comme les Etats-Unis, où les opinions ne diffèrent que par les nuances, le droit d'association peut rester pour ainsi dire sans limites*'. Ibid., II, 40–1.
15. '*à proportion que le peuple devient propriétaire . . . le peuple a moins besoin de l'argent des riches*'. Ibid., II, 71.
16. '*hommes puissants et éclairés*'; '*ils ne présentent point d'individus semblables*'; '*les hommes les plus capables de gouverner*'. Ibid., II, 46–8.
17. '*les lumières, disaient-ils, sont les seules garanties que nous ayons contre les écarts de la multitude.*' Ibid.
18. '*Il s'agit bien moins pour les partisans de la démocratie de faire gouverner le peuple, que de faire choisir au peuple les hommes les plus capables de gouverner, et de lui donner sur ceux-là un empire assez grand pour qu'il puisse diriger l'ensemble de leur conduite, et non le détail des actes, ni les moyens d'exécution. Tel est le problème. Je suis parfaitement convaincu que de sa solution dépend le sort des nations modernes. Mais combien peu de gens même l'aperçoivent! Combien peu le signalent!*' Unpublished letter to J. S. Mill, Tocqueville, June 1835.
19. '*ce qui est juste*'. *OE. C.* II, 142. *De la Démocratie en Amérique.*

20 Ibid., I, 256.

21 Ibid., II, 145.

22 '*Ces pouvoirs illimités … on pouvait être amené à les lui concéder lorsqu'il semblait représenter la souveraineté nationale; et c'est ainsi que Napoléon put enfin dire sans trop blesser le sens public, qu'il avait le droit de tout commander parce que seul il parlait au nom du peuple.*' *OE. C.* IX, 14. '*Discours à l'Académie Française*', 21.4.1842.

23 *OE.C.* II, 54. *De la Démocratie en Amérique.*

24 Ibid., II, 47.

25 Quoted in Mayer, op. cit., p. 86.

26 Ibid., p. 118.

27 '*c'est là une expression magnifique.*' *OE.C.* III, 205. *De la Démocratie en Amérique.*

28 Mayer, op. cit., p. 118.

29 Ibid.

30 '*tendance naturelle pour centraliser le pouvoir.*' *OE. C.* VIII, 34. '*Etat Social et Politique de la France avant et depuis 1789*'.

31 K. Marx: *The Civil War in France,* p. 37.

32 '*Je pense qu'on ne saurait donner impunément aux hommes une grande alternative de force et de faiblesse, leur faire toucher l'extrême égalité sur un point, et les laisser souffrir de l'extrême inégalité sur les autres, sans que bientôt ils n'aspirent à être forts, ou ne deviennent faibles sur tous.*' *OE. C.* VIII, 29. '*Etat Social et Politique de la France avant et depuis 1789*'.

33 '*l'industrie pourrait bien à son tour ramener les hommes vers l'aristocratie.*' Ibid. III, 258ff.

34 Ibid., III, 258.

35 '*une théorie industrielle … l'attache à un métier, et souvent à un lieu qu'il ne peut quitter … Elle lui a assigné dans la société une certaine place dont il ne peut sortir*'. Ibid.

36 Ibid., III, 288–98.

37 '*l'obéissance perd sa moralité aux yeux de celui qui obéit … elle n'est à ses yeux ni sainte ni juste*'. Ibid., 298.

38 '*Bientôt, il n'y en a guère à s'en douter, c'est entre ceux qui possèdent et ceux qui ne possèdent pas que s'établira la lutte des partis politiques … et les principales questions de la politique rouleront sur des modifications plus ou moins profondes à apporter au droit des propriétaires.*' *OE. C.* IX, 517. '*De la Classe Moyenne et du Peuple*'.

39 e.g. H. J. Laski, *Alexis de Tocqueville and Democracy.*

40 *OE.C.* III, 298. *De la Démocratie en Amérique.*

41 *OE.C.* IX, 535. Speech to Chamber of Deputies, 27.1.1848.

42 '*l'esprit humain perdit entièrement son assiette*'; '*portèrent l'audace jusqu'à la folie, qu'aucune nouveauté ne put surprendre, aucun scrupule ralentir, et qui n'hésitèrent jamais devant l'exécution d'aucun dessein*'. *OE. C.* V, 230–1. *L'Ancien Régime.*

43 *OE. C.* IX, 420–1. Speech to Chamber of Deputies, 28.4.1845.

44 '*si la liberté se sépare d'une manière définitive et complète des croyances … il lui manquera toujours cet élément de … stabilité, de tranquillité, de vie, qui seul la rend grande et féconde*'. Ibid., 421–2.

# CHAPTER IV
## The Test

In *L'Avenir de la France*, Renan, writing in 1848, describes a flock of sheep in his native Brittany, each sheep tied to a pole in the middle of the flock, and able to feed only on the limited amount of grass within its reach. This fatal helplessness, this inability to go outside a restricted radius reminded him of the French thinkers of his period. This striking image reminds us of Tocqueville, tied by his personal sympathies and his ideal to the pole of liberalism, and unable either to see the merits of socialism or to prevent despotism. This helplessness gave rise to an inner conflict, which was brought to a climax by the struggle for power between the left wing and the right wing in the revolution of 1848. If we examine his reactions to the events between 1848 and 1852 we shall be able to determine the strength of his attachment to his chosen ideal and its effectiveness in an exacting test.

On February 24th 1848, a fusillade of bullets abruptly ended a generation of social peace. Tocqueville's *'vent des révolutions'* [revolutionary wind] had descended from the clouds and struck the earth. With an audacity which astonished and alarmed the intelligentsia, the Provisional Government introduced a full democratic constitution—universal franchise, liberty of the press, liberty of association and an elected President. Tocqueville's ideal was to be put to the test: would the people use their liberties to do what was good and just, or prove themselves to be incapable of exercising the responsibilities they had assumed? If we limited our inquiry to the legislation of the Provisional Government we should expect Tocqueville to approve of their work. Certainly their social legislation corresponded with the recommendations in his speeches and writings. The condition of the working classes received their sympathetic attention. They appointed a special Commission to draw up plans for the realisation of this ideal. Wages, working hours, living conditions—all these symptoms of working-class misery were to come within the scope of their work. As proof of their intention to act upon the recommendations of this Commission, the Government on March 3rd issued a decree reducing the working day in Paris by one hour, while in the same month decrees to abolish abuses in subcontracting—the main cause of sweated labour—were gazetted.[1]

Nor could a man with his ideal take exception to either the aims or the methods of the Minister responsible for the material well-being of the working classes—Louis Blanc. Indeed the sentiments in his Manifesto might well have been written by Tocqueville. There was to be 'the greatest enlightenment obtainable, in order that our work of justice should be begun in impartiality'. He favoured economic equality because it is 'a principle of order that excludes hatred and jealousy'. He, too, was searching for the economic conditions which would make hatred, wars and revolutions forever impossible. He did not propose to use compulsion in the building of his social utopia. 'No one was to be treated with violence . . . the private companies, the present economic system would live on side by side with the publicly owned factories. Men will perceive the superior qualities of his system; they will be drawn to it by an irresistible power of attraction.'[2] To implement this policy, Louis Blanc established three co-operative factories—for tailors, saddlers and spinners.

That was in March of 1848. By May of the same year the Government had begun to pass legislation designed to ensure a more equal distribution of wealth. Progressive taxes were imposed on high incomes and the money raised distributed among the necessitous—precisely Tocqueville's suggestion. This work was not carried out by men who were crass materialists. It was the work of men who were inspired by the very ideals which warmed the breast of Tocqueville. They spoke of 'justice', of liberty, of equality and fraternity, of the civilising mission of their government.[3] Indeed their leader, Alphonse Lamartine, was so much an exponent of the idealist's approach that the Paris mob of May 15th 1848, intent on bread and not silver words, silenced him with the cry *'Plus de lyre!'* [No more poetry!] Men who dreamed of harmony on earth would have found themselves in congenial company if they had visited the Hôtel de Ville in Paris during its occupation by the Provisional Government.

Yet, from the first, Tocqueville did not share the enthusiasm of those who hailed the fall of Guizot as the beginning of the millennium. The only record of his reactions—*Souvenirs*—contains not one word of approval for the work of the Second Republic. It is admittedly an acid work: the King and his Ministers are castigated with equal severity, while Louis Napoleon and his supporters are contemptuously dismissed as gangsters and confidence tricksters. Still, his disapproval of them is intelligible. What is not quite so self-evident is the reason for his opposition to the Provisional Government. After all, they were trying to do what he had recommended —that is, from his study! But perhaps the attachment to the ideal was not strong enough to bear the strain of an exacting test. His belief in equality was no more than an 'intellectual taste'. We shall see in a moment how strong such attachments are when the heart is distressed.

Nor will the superficial reasons for his disapproval account for the nervous anxiety which is his prevailing mood in *Souvenirs*. He preferred a hereditary monarch as the head of the executive: the Revolution had expelled the Bourbons ignominiously and was committed to a republican constitution. Still, this was not a fundamental issue, and besides, he himself had prophesied the advent of a republic: 'I have always held that the future of France lay with democratic and republican institutions'.[4] He wanted the franchise to be extended gradually, after the disfranchised had served their apprenticeship in the work-shop of political knowledge—local government—and had proved their capacity to use their liberties properly.[5] The Revolution ignored these arguments for a gradual change. He also disapproved of all political changes achieved by violence or the threat to use violence. For this reason he had refused the invitation to be present at the political banquets held as demonstrations against the Guizot régime. This is a crucial objection: if applied literally it would invalidate the claim of the bourgeois monarchy, which was, in its turn, a child of the barricades. But Tocqueville accepted Louis Philippe contrary to his conscience and he accepted the Provisional Government too as a *fait accompli.*

Nor was the Provisional Government over-attentive to his demand for the reconciliation between the Church and the supporters of liberty. For liberty they professed the same ardent affection as he himself, but they were, like most liberals and socialists of that time, suspicious of the political activities of the Church and anxious to restrict its activities to religious questions. The Church quaintly called this policy 'persecution' and denounced the Republicans as the agents of the anti-Christ. Indeed this clash was also a fulfilment of his thesis that the Church becomes vindictive and spiteful whenever social or political progress rears its head, to which the supporters of these movements can only retaliate by restricting its activities. Yet he preserves a significant silence on this unedifying spectacle. Perhaps he was too disgusted with the Church's behaviour; at any rate, he does not join in their heresy hunt against the Government.

For the real reasons for his disapproval we must examine the pages of *Souvenirs*. And what a strange book it is! A text-book on the causes of the Revolution, observations on the philosophy of history and a diary of his own experiences. The significant point is that the personal record is much more detailed for the first six months, February to June 1848, than for the last three and a half years—June 1848 to December 1851. The events of these first six months evidently made a very strong impression—even after the lapse of two years he could still recall the personal appearance and the gestures of the men he saw then for the first and last time. The experiences of May to June 1848 obviously imposed an emotional strain in which he lost sight of his ideal. To begin with, he had no personal bond with the men who made the Revolution. He evidently felt it was his duty to make their acquaintance—'I am forever asking the names of these unknowns (revealing word!) whom I see every day'[6] —but he forgot them as soon as he had left them. The men with the 'great hearts' to whom he had warmed in the salons of Paris, or invited to the family estate at Tocqueville, were in eclipse. The Second Republic attracted the mediocrities, 'the unknowns'.[k] Why should a man with his tastes and accomplishments be enthusiastic about these men who bored him profoundly?[7]

Boredom explains the frozen heart; it does not explain his anger with the supporters of the régime. For that we must notice his opinion on their values. Here a familiar theme is played—these people are rabid materialists. The most casual conversations are produced as evidence for this judgement. A working-class girl from one of the industrial *faubourgs* [suburbs] is asked to express an opinion on the Revolution. Her reply shocked and disgusted him: 'we'll be the ones eating the chickens' wings now!'[8] The fantasies of an undernourished girl are taken to be typical of the movement. How different, he thought, from the revolution of 1789: 'The revolution of 1789 sprang from the brain and the heart of the nation, but this one was in part conceived in its stomach'.[9] But the writings of the 'superior individuals' are sprinkled with sentiments similar to those of the working girl. An idea loses its grossness in proportion to the elegance with which it is presented. Burke may boast that no gentleman has ever been obliged to retrench one dish at his table through any measure of his. To this Tocqueville would not object; but to desire to eat the wings of a fowl is to be coarse and disgusting. Evidently it all depends on the appearance of the person and the language in which the desire is clothed.

Certainly the coarse dress and simple toilet of the Montagnards were a great shock to him. On the 15th May 1848 he saw [Louis] Blanqui for the first time. His impressions were that the man seemed to have lived in a sewer and to have left it only to attend the Assembly. Blanqui exhorted the Assembly to abolish poverty and misery—the blot on Parisian society. But Tocqueville simply cannot warm to the man, despite the community of ideals. What impressed him was his personal appearance—'the very memory of the man has always filled me with horror and disgust'.[10] There is abundant

---

[k]   On p. 88 of the copy text, Clark inserts a marginal note: 'What about Lamartine?'

evidence in *Souvenirs* that the reasons for his disapproval of the Revolution are not the aims of the parties but the type of people supporting these movements. Blanqui and George Sand had similar ideals. Blanqui filled him with disgust and horror: he spent a pleasant evening with George Sand—one of the very few times that he felt at ease during the whole revolution.[11]

He does not reject the social theories of these people by the a priori argument that what has been must continue in the future. On the contrary, he is prepared to admit that great social changes are distinctly possible: 'those institutions which we call necessary are often simply those to which we are accustomed, and where social organisation is concerned, the field of the possible is much vaster than those living in any particular society imagine'.[12] But the detachment of the study fades before the grim reality of the barricade. The dregs attracted by every revolutionary movement disgust and alarm him. In this state of alarm a new scale of values determines his behaviour. The criterion of a man's worth is the appearance of his collar. Blanqui wore a dirty one. Here then was a new situation for an idealist. The man who had recommended his contemporaries to subdue their personal antipathy to the behaviour of the bourgeoisie was overwhelmed by the first dirty collar he saw.

The interesting effect of this emotional upheaval is the significant part which it plays as a motive governing his conduct during the revolutionary period. Indeed, the issues uppermost in his mind before the Revolution seem to be almost extinguished by the avalanche of June 1848. There is a solitary lugubrious reference to the fate of liberty—'liberty is irretrievably lost'[13]—but there are no observations on the use of the liberties, nor does he regret the absence of religion as a restraint upon the behaviour of the working classes. What is even more remarkable is the complete absence of any reference to his ideal in the sentence in which he summed up what he believed was worth defending from the deluge: 'I decided to plunge headlong into the arena and to risk my fortune, my security and my person in the defence not of a particular government, but of the laws on which society itself is based'.[14] We might have expected his belief in equality—a mere '*goût de tête*' [intellectual taste]—to be jettisoned; but even liberty, '*le premier des biens*' [the primary good], is sacrificed to deal with the greater evil.

The irony of the situation was that this aim could be achieved only by association with the very men whom he despised: the petty bourgeois Jacobins, scared by the socialist threat to private property, and bound hand and foot to the Bourse,[15] the '*petit pot au feu bourgeois*' [petty stay-at-home bourgeois] who bored and disgusted him; the Carlists, the men of his own social class, whose political values he had repudiated after the American journey; the doctrinaire Republicans, the lawyers, journalists, university professors—the timid souls who loved The People from the shelter of the study or the salon, but found them to be monsters on the barricade. Even if they were personally unattractive, their aims were substantially the same as his: 'Defence of Property, Religion and the Family', while their contribution to the suppression of the June rising was proof both of their determination and their power to subdue the main cause of his disquiet, 'the chaotic actions of the masses, their violent and ignorant intervention in public affairs'.[16]

After the suppression of the June rising, the rudiments of the original ideal reappear, but so circumscribed as to be almost unrecognisable. There is a faint bleat for liberty—it must be saved—but equality has faded from his mind, being too redolent of the painful and distressing scenes on the barricades. The significant point is that the recommendations he makes after the June rising conflict with the methods suggested in *De la Démocratie en Amérique*. The ideal is put aside in the crisis: principle succumbs to the pressing need to suppress the mob. In a test case he finds order to be a greater good than liberty. The odd thing is that in 1835 he was sneering at the bourgeois for having precisely the same values—was not the man who preferred '*le bon ordre*' to liberty a slave to his passions? But to restore order, Tocqueville was now prepared to eat the very words with which he had defined his creed: men had the power to choose the conditions under which they would live within the limits defined by God. Anyone who maintained that man was denied this freedom of choice by economic laws, physical features or climate was using the language of slavery.

But here were men like Blanqui, Blanc and Rollin, using this power to choose to persuade working men of the possibility of creating a socialist society in which wealth would be equally distributed. To silence this demand, or rather to persuade working men that their aims were unattainable, Tocqueville denies the very principle he had so stoutly defended in the thirties. He writes in support of the proposal by the 'Académie des Sciences Morales et Politiques' to distribute text-books on political economy amongst the working classes—evidently the middle and upper classes were not in need of instruction. The aim of these text-books was to educate the working classes in the most elementary principles of political economy. The very first was a repudiation of the principles of liberty. The workers must understand the eternal economic laws which determined the wage scale—indeed these laws and the 'structure of society' were unalterable because they represented the nature of man and were therefore divine. Curious that the deity should be trotted out to justify the poverty and misery of the working man.

But then, possibly scenting working-class suspicion of the religious argument, he likens these economic laws to the laws of nature: the government can no more raise the wage of a working man when the demand for labour decreases than a man can prevent water from 'spreading in the direction the glass is tilted'.[17] We agree that determinism is the language of slavery, but what could be worse than the grinding poverty of the sweated labourers of Paris and the other towns of France? Yet if men accepted his teaching, this economic slavery would be perpetual. These sentiments were admittedly the product of the mood of the moment; neither before nor after the Revolution does he use such language. Indeed, within two years, when the spectre of the barricade had receded, and the 'cool head' could reflect undisturbed by the horrors of street fighting, he had reverted to his original opinions on social organisation: 'I have no doubt that the laws governing our modern society will be greatly modified in the long run'.[18] Nor did these sentiments have much effect. The members of the Academy might applaud, but the workers would find more appropriate use for the paper on which they were written!

But the methods he supported for the preservation of liberty had important and far-reaching results. To save liberty, restrictions must be placed on the use of the liberties. So long as these restrictions apply only to liberty of association, there is nothing inconsistent between this position and the conclusions reached in *De la Démocratie en Amérique*. But the experience of 1848 has introduced a new factor into the discussion. Society has an imprescriptible right to save itself. No right of the individual can stand between society and this sacred right.[19] We may ask: save itself from what? And the reply would be: from such events as the demonstration on the Champ de Mars in April 1848, from the invasion of the Assembly in May 1848, from the street fighting of June 1848. In other words, the 'disturbances' which terrified the bourgeois into support of any government which could guarantee order had a similar effect on this 'superior individual'. So the repressive measures of the Barrot Ministry—the suppression of the political clubs and the censorship of the press—are justified because 'after such a violent revolution the only remaining means of saving liberty was to restrict it'.[20] Restriction, not total suppression—thus the ideal is whittled away.

Nor was he completely free from the temptation which he had prophesied would induce the weaker spirits to abandon liberty—the use of the strong man. In the first presidential election, he voted for General Cavaignac[21]—the butcher of the barricades, and candidate of the 'Party of Order'. In 1849 and 1850 he toyed with the idea of using Louis Napoleon to restore order and then discarding him when he had performed this service. For this reason he became a minister in the government of Odilon Barrot. He also tried to persuade his colleagues in the National Assembly to amend the clause in the constitution which forbade a President to seek re-election.[22] The idea was to appease Louis Napoleon by conceding half his demands voluntarily, and thus prevent a violent *coup d'état*.

Here was a crucial test: expediency dictated a modification of his ideal, a compromise with Satan to achieve a desirable result. But Satan too makes use of the compromise, and the result is personally unpleasant—Tocqueville was arrested later by Louis Napoleon—and, fatal to the ideal, Louis Napoleon suppressed <u>all</u> the liberties.

To revert to the image with which we began the chapter: if the ideal, like the pole to which the sheep were tied, was a restriction upon his freedom of action, then at the first serious test he was anxious to abandon it, if not entirely, then sufficiently to make it worthless as a security against the big bad wolf of despotism.

An idealist who had become frightened—this is perhaps the strongest impression left by *Souvenirs*. Tocqueville was of course not the only renegade in the idealist camp. The horrors of the June days, the fear of a more violent and bloody revolution disposed men's minds to clutch at straws, to jettison their ideals for the preservation of order. Proudhon tells us: 'I fled before the monster of democratic socialism, the riddle of which I could not unravel; and an inexpressible terror froze my soul, depriving me of every thought'.[23] From Walter Bagehot we learn of the anxiety of the Parisians, and the relief when the *coup d'état* banished the spectre of street fighting. 'In France, five weeks ago (he was writing in 1852), the tradespeople talked of May 1852 as if it were the end of the world . . . Six weeks ago society was living from hand to mouth; now she feels sure of her next meal. And this, in a dozen words is the real case—the political excuse for Prince Louis Napoleon.'[24]

But it is just the idealists and the men who are indifferent to all considerations except peace and a full stomach who panic as soon as the tocsin sounds. It is the Lamartines with their doctrines of fraternity as the solvent for the 'terrible misunderstanding between the classes',[25] the Cavaignacs with their conviction that the workers are not only brutal but sinful—('Come to us as <u>repentant</u> brothers, submitting to the law; the arms of the Republic are open to receive you'[26]); the Proudhons with their belief that love elevates a man's mind above the class struggle: these are the men who are often the shrillest in their appeal for order when the workers wake up from the stupor induced by their sentiments and take to the barricades. Moreover, it is just these idealists who believe that an appeal to the heart will turn the minds of their antagonists from their evil ways and bring them back into the way of peace. During the street fighting in June 1848, the Archbishop of Paris courageously walked into the working-class district to effect a reconciliation between the two sides. He was accidentally shot down before he had taken ten paces.[27] It was events such as this which inspired Viennet to write an epigrammatic poem deriding the ideals of the workers:

> *Liberté de mourir de faim;*
> *Egalité en misère;*
> *Fraternité de Cain.*[28]
>
> [Liberty to starve to death,
> Equality in want;
> Fraternity of Cain.]

There are passages in *Souvenirs* in which his description of the working men and their values does not fall far short of this biting indictment. Was not the motive of the working class base? Was not Blanqui one of the scum of the earth? Did he not attend the Feast of Fraternity at the Place de la Concorde with a pistol under his coat? Indeed, the modern reader who is familiar with the lives and aims of these working-class leaders, and the fervent denunciation of them by their opponents, may be tempted to accept Lamartine's judgement that it was a '*malentendu terrible*' [terrible misunderstanding]. Like Proudhon, those men wrote of happiness, of justice and of fraternity; like Cavaignac they appealed in the name of humanity. Both groups wanted the good life, and as between Tocqueville, Proudhon, Blanc, Barbès, Lamartine and Rollin, there was substantial agreement in their definition of that life.

Nor, as we have seen, did Tocqueville disapprove of these men so long as they were refined and polite. It is their supporters who rouse his antagonism. It is in their presence that the ideals which made him weep for joy in the silence of his study grow dim as he wanders past the cafés, through the streets, the squares and the barricades. Perhaps he was too sensitive, too squeamish to tolerate the coarseness of the workman. Perhaps, too, the workman was imprudent to offend the sensibilities of the intelligentsia. After all, the heart of both sides was in the right place. One was exquisite, the other crude; one subtle, the other naive. It is easy to sketch the differences. But perhaps if Tocqueville had exercised more self-discipline he might have felt sympathy and compassion with the girl who quaintly yearned for the wings of a pullet. He might even have felt sorry that poverty compelled Blanqui to wear a dirty collar. But if fraternity is a stimulant for reconciliation Tocqueville must have drunk a very sour brand. Not only his teeth were on edge; his mind too was antagonistic to these men who dreamed of a new heaven on earth.

His evaluation of the socialists presents a curious paradox. Fear and contempt for the supporters justify suppression even at the expense of the ideal, while the mind rejects their theories because they are incompatible with his ideal. The discussion of their theories is not conducted in language which suggests that his judgement has been perverted by the painful experiences on the barricades. So long as he is posing the empirical question: 'Why do working men believe in socialism?' the 'cool head' can work free of the 'burning passions'. It is when he asks the ethical question: 'Are they right to believe in socialism?' that the mind is not a free agent.

The answer to the first question begins with the economic causes. In the second quarter of the nineteenth century the economic condition of the workers in France had not improved commensurately with their progress in importance, in enlightenment and power. At the same time, their faith in an afterlife, which had enabled them to endure their misery in this world, became less. Their misery became the more intolerable as the vision of a blessed relief faded from their minds. The problem was how to rid themselves of this burden of poverty. Their first method was to change all the existing political institutions, but after each change they found that their lot had either not improved at all, or very, very slowly.

So it was inevitable that the people would sooner or later discover that what bound them to their position was not the constitution of the government but the immutable laws of social organisation. It was natural that they should go on to ask whether they had the power and the right to change these laws just as they had changed the political laws. All other privileges in society had been destroyed; why should they not abolish private property, the sole surviving obstacle to equality? Was it not natural, if not to abolish that institution, then at least that the idea of abolishing it should occur to the minds of those who did not enjoy its benefits?[29] The supporters of this idea may be monstrous and grotesque, the works in which they presented their ideas 'ridiculous', but the basis on which this idea is founded is 'the most serious issue which philosophers and statesmen can address'.[30] Nor can he see any objection in theory to the idea of abolishing private property: forms of private property vary from age to age. Had not the French Revolution itself made a sweeping change in the distribution of property?

But if the mind can find no objections to the demand for a modification of the social system, he must still ask: are these changes compatible with my ideal? Once again it is illuminating to revert to the image of the sheep tethered to the pole in the centre of the flock. The eye perceives fresh pastures, but the pole determines its attitude to them. Or is it that the heart is so revolted by the visual impression of these fresh pastures that mind and ideal merely justify the heart's affection? At least there is a great change in the tone and mood of the discussion as he moves from the empirical question of causation to the ethical one: ought we to accept the socialist solution? If the ideal is the criterion by which he answers the question, the mind does not object to contradictions in the arguments by which he justifies his belief in the possibility of social change.

Significantly enough, the refutation of the socialist theory begins with a tirade against its values. The most striking quality in socialist philosophy is the persistent and energetic appeal to the materialist passions of mankind.[31] The evidence for his opinion is contained in the socialist slogans: '*Qu'il s'agissait de réhabiliter la chair*' [the body must come back into its own], and '*Qu'il fallait que le travail même le plus dur, ne fût pas seulement utile, mais agréable*' [Even the most arduous labour must be not only useful but pleasant].[32] It is a question of the type of appeal made to men. The French Revolutionaries [of 1789] inspired their contemporaries to great actions not by speaking about their salaries, their well-being or the satisfaction of their physical needs, but by discussing 'loftier and finer things. It was by speaking of their native land . . . of virtue, generosity, altruism and glory that the Revolution achieved great things'.[33]

Empirically, of course, he may be right: men may be more responsive to an appeal to their 'higher nature', they may be persuaded not only to endure material hardship but to sacrifice their lives in the defence of an ideal. But the socialists themselves were not destitute of those qualities of self-sacrifice, courage, generous sentiments and visions of harmony which he maintained would be extinguished by their doctrines. The socialists dreamed not only of a more equal distribution of wealth, but of a society conducive to the highest development of man—a dream for which they believed no sacrifice to be too great: 'In times to come, no man will kill another, the earth will shine, the human race will be full of love. The day will come when all will be concord, harmony, light, joy and life. It is coming! And it is to ensure its coming that we are to die'.[34]

There is nothing 'materialist' in this ideal. The point was that the socialists insisted that the good life could not be pursued by all until they were freed from the anxieties and drudgery of satisfying their material needs under the previous harsh conditions. For Tocqueville this was evidence of their addiction to what we might call the 'materialist bogey'. What he objected to was the opinion that the higher pleasures, to put it crudely, depend on a full stomach. He never recommends an empty or a half-empty stomach as a healthy discipline. On the contrary, as we shall see, he wanted all men to have a sufficiency of this world's goods. But unless men insist that justice means good wages, good living conditions, how will they be achieved? If the ideal excludes all reference to material satisfactions, may not all demands for improvement in economic conditions be condemned as incompatible with it?

Moreover, the men who are reluctant to use the language of the materialists are generally the most hysterical whenever any party or government passes legislation to secure a more even distribution of wealth, which might adversely affect the incomes of their own class. Indeed, what the poor have to expect from the idealists is not only a prohibition against trespassing on the green pastures of material well-being, but also a reproach that to trespass is a mark of a vicious nature. This is perhaps the strongest weapon they have: to arouse feelings of guilt in their opponents, and to make renunciation of their material desires the condition of their atonement. The emancipation of the working classes depends on their power to be unashamed of their aims! Until they achieve this, they will always be vulnerable to the type of appeal made by Cavaignac—'come to us as <u>repentant</u> brothers; the arms of the Republic are open to receive you'.[35] Unless of course they come to believe that the guilt feeling is more tolerable than the upper-class idea of 'atonement'—at that time exile in Cayenne (in our time the 're-education' of the concentration camps).

The second objection to the socialists is their attitude to private property. The socialists believed that private property was the cause of all the evil in the world, that private property was theft.[36] Hence some of them wanted to abolish it, while others wanted to diminish its evil effects by controlling the activities of the owners.[37] This argument of the socialists is refuted not as immoral—Tocqueville called it *'franche et un peu brutale'* [honest and somewhat brutal] —but on the grounds that private property is the only form of property known since the beginning of the world. This may reassure defenders of the institution (*Le Moniteur* records that there were 'Emphatic expressions of agreement'[38]) but it is unconvincing to those for whom the practices of the past are not an unquestionable sanction for behaviour in the present or the future.

But even Tocqueville himself did not subscribe to this opinion in calmer moments. He knew there had been other forms of property. Bad history was an unusual fault with him. This argument was used in September 1848 when the spectre of the *drapeau rouge* [red flag] was still haunting his mind. Two years later his mind was reflecting on 'the different forms taken by the right to property in world history, whatever may be said to the contrary'.[39] Even in September 1848 the argument is used rather as a debating point. At least he follows a sound maxim in debating tactics: when the case is weak, resort to ridicule. And what could be more ridiculous than a desire to change an institution which had existed since the beginning of recorded history?

If the argument from history was little more than a rhetorical *tour de force*, there is a grim earnestness in the third and final objection to socialism—its 'profound mistrust of liberty'.[40] Liberty, by his definition, means free choice—an opportunity to decide, without compulsion, the conditions of one's life. The democracy which he believed in 'extends the sphere of individual independence', but socialism 'restricts it'.[41] And why? Because in a socialist society, the State assumes the responsibility for the welfare of the individual. The State becomes the tutor and ruler of each individual; it is the function of the State 'to surround him, in order to guide him, protect him, maintain him and restrain him'.[42] If the State exercised such powers, the ideal which he had espoused—a society of free and civilised men—would be unattainable. Instead there would be a society of animals, a society for bees and beavers.[43]

The Marxist may reply to this argument that only a socialist society can create the conditions favourable to the pursuit of liberty. Did not Marx himself make a pronouncement on this subject: 'An association in which the free development of each is the condition for the free development of all'. Let the hot-headed pause before they don the black cap to pass judgement on the orthodoxy of the writer. Most of the muddled arguments on socialism and liberty can be disentangled by observing carefully the definition of both these terms. Tocqueville's definition is: if the state compels an individual to pursue a definite occupation, to hold one set of opinions to the exclusion of another, liberty has been restricted. We may aspire to create a society in which men <u>voluntarily</u> perform the task allotted to them, but so far there is no evidence that men will either voluntarily surrender their economic privileges, or undertake work which is repugnant to them. Compulsion may be unpleasant; its opponents are assured of a sympathetic hearing. But approval of the ideal must be qualified by an examination of its consequences.

If the liberty of the capitalist is unrestricted, the consequences are wealth for the very few and poverty for the many—and not only poverty but also unemployment with its attendant evils, death by starvation, or crime to procure a subsistence. Tocqueville's answer to this would be to eliminate starvation but not poverty. The State should come to the assistance of those who were in dire need, of those who, after exhausting their own resources, would starve without State assistance. Any extension of the State's powers and responsibilities beyond the duty to administer charity in necessitous cases was an infringement of liberty.[44] In other words, no-one is to die because assistance would have deprived him of his liberty, but men may suffer economic hardship, the distribution of wealth may be grossly unequal—a potent cause, as he himself had insisted, of social unrest. Still Tocqueville is adamant: State interference is incompatible with liberty. To preserve liberty, men must wait patiently until the desired economic changes can be achieved without interference by the State, and without compulsion. The consequences of pursuing Tocqueville's ideal of liberty are opposition to the only possible methods of changing an unjust distribution of wealth. The effects of applying this ideal to society are similar to the effects of his opposition to the materialists—pious intentions with shocking results.

Here then is a dilemma. So long as the workers accept socialist ideas they will not use the liberties to do what is good and just. On the other hand, so long as they are poor they will accept socialism as the way out of their misery. What is to be done? Here is a test case for the methods by which a majority may be corrected when in error. The legislator, it will be recalled (see above, Chapter III), must be guided not by popular passions but by the law of justice. In practice this meant restrictions on the liberties of the people until these desires had been curbed and abandoned. And, as we have noticed before, Tocqueville advocated the suppression of political clubs and the censorship of the press as expedients by which to prevent men from encouraging these evil desires. At the same time, he supported proposals to distribute literature amongst the working classes to correct their erroneous opinions. Undoubtedly his arguments for restriction were sincere. He wanted to restore the liberties as soon as the workers had abandoned their socialist theories. The motive for the restriction was not to maintain the political and economic power of a minority, but to guarantee that all men would desire '*ce qui est bon et juste*' [that which is good and just].

But although the motive may have been disinterested, in practice restriction was imposed by a party which was acting on very different motives. The bourgeois perceived that the exercise of political liberty jeopardised his economic privileges. He saw his 'purchases and sales, his bills of exchange, his marriages, his legal contracts, his mortgages, his ground rents, house rents, profits, all his contracts and sources of gain called in question' by the votes of working men, and he could not expose himself to this risk.[45] In other words, the bourgeois understood that all the so-called bourgeois liberties and organs of progress attacked the rule of his own class at its very foundations, and its political summit simultaneously.[46] For these reasons they were prepared to support any government which would 'weaken the authority of universal suffrage'.[47]

And because their main fear was of the anarchy, chaos and civil war produced by universal suffrage, the bourgeois welcomed wholeheartedly Louis Napoleon's assurance: 'I promise you <u>tranquillity</u> for the future'.[48] Tocqueville was not unaware of the motives of these men. Their leading motive, he tells us, was the preservation of their material well-being. For this, they were prepared to approve of any form of government provided it permitted them to accumulate wealth.[49] What he wanted was a temporary restraint upon the liberties of the individual, to wean the workers away from their faith in socialism. What occurred was the ruthless suppression of the liberties, by men whose behaviour and values were as repulsive to him as the men and the theory they were repressing.

Tocqueville had wanted a restriction of the liberties as a temporary expedient. Louis Napoleon totally suppressed the liberties of the individual and evinced a painful indifference to the demands for their restitution: 'The liberty of the press is destroyed to an extent unheard of even in the time of the Empire . . . Human life is as little respected as human liberty . . . Force overturning law, trampling on the liberty of the press and of the person, deriding the popular will'.[50] He had wanted these restrictions to be imposed by men of high character and superior attainments, men who would be unafraid and unmoved by the abuse levelled at them by the people whose evil desires they were frustrating. Neither the leader nor his supporters measured up to these standards. The leader, Louis Napoleon, was selfish, vain, cowardly, capricious—a foreigner by birth and education. (Are we to assume that only a Frenchman could perform such an exacting task?) His supporters too were vile and contemptible—'a set of military ruffians, and of infamous civilians, fit only to have formed the staff and the privy council of Catiline'.[51] Indeed in the whole of France only three men who enjoyed the

respect and esteem of the 'superior individuals' were active supporters of the régime—Montalembert, an ultramontane; Baroche, a
country lawyer; and Fould, a Jewish banker.[52]

He had wanted restriction to lead men back to the cultivation
of desirable activities; the restrictions were used to pursue *de petits
et vulgaires plaisirs* [petty and vulgar pleasures] and the most important of these was the accumulation of wealth.[53] True, their resistance
to the socialists had been effective. The socialist leaders and their
supporters were either in exile or deprived of all means of influencing their contemporaries, except by underground activities. But
once this mission was fulfilled, would they restore the liberties
essential for the pursuit of his ideal? And if not, how could the
group in power be removed?

The answer to this crucial question depended on the strength
of the resistance to Louis Napoleon—now Napoleon III—a strength
determined by the number of people who disapproved of his conduct. Active resistance was negligible. What was even more distressing was the small number who objected to the régime. Dissatisfaction
was confined almost entirely to the educated classes—the men who
could not bear to be deprived of the pleasure of expressing their
opinions without fear of the consequences. The behaviour of the
majority both before and after the *coup d'état* was a grim testimony
to their indifference to Tocqueville's values. Though this behaviour
was a fulfilment of his earlier prophecies (Nassau Senior wrote:
'Your conversations have so much prepared me for the events which
have passed since May, that I seem to be looking at a play which I
have read in manuscript'[54]) the event itself plunged him into the
depths of depression—'I should indeed be distressed to be less sad',
he told his friend Beaumont, 'for I am sad unto death'.[55]

The feeble opposition to Napoleon III, the indifference of the
masses to the shocking and brutal methods used by his satellites to
suppress the heroic few who resisted: was not this evidence that the
masses were incapable of pursuing the life of the 'superior individuals'? Even England, the grand jury of the world in the cause
of freedom, was inclined to overlook the crimes against liberty.
Her Foreign Minister had given formal recognition to Napoleon's
Government without even a bleat for liberty. For Schwarzenberg,

the Austrian Chancellor, the sole reason for recognising Napoleon was that he was a more effective bulwark against liberty than the Orleans or elder branch of the House of Bourbon who had 'parliamentary leanings'. Indeed, Napoleon's great service in Schwarzenberg's eyes was his suppression of 'parliamentarianism'.[56]

So as Tocqueville watched the behaviour of his contemporaries during his sojourn at Sorrento, or from the seclusion of Tocqueville, and saw that even so-called liberals such as Thiers and Guizot abandoned their opposition and became reconciled to the régime, while even his intimate friends such as Beaumont and Kergorlay repressed their feelings so as not to give offence, he saw how this torpor became more profound from day to day, making effective opposition more and more impossible.[57] There was but one conclusion to draw from these observations: his contemporaries had no affection for his ideal, or, as he put it: 'they no longer attach importance to the values to which my whole heart remains devoted'.[58]

He did not attempt to delude himself about the effect of this absence of devotion to his values. The cause of liberty *'est perdue sans ressource'* [is lost beyond recall]. Hence his gloom, his willingness to die. Why regret separation from men who did not share his thoughts?[59] The most searching test of a man's attachment to an ideal is his reaction when he is deprived of the means of pursuing it. Frenchmen were so indifferent to the liberties that they not only failed to resist their suppression but forgot them almost immediately after the *coup d'état*. 'One might think that there never had been any liberal institutions in France to judge by the astonishment aroused when one speaks of them to people';[60] that was his impression in April 1852. The significant quality in his mood after December 1851 is that the stronger the conviction became that his ideal was unattainable, the more he affirmed his belief in it. The vision of what he wanted became clearer as his expectation of its realisation dwindled. Even in 1858, one year before his death, the vision was constantly floating before his eyes. But liberty, as he conceived it, was unattainable. France might revive her liberal institutions, but they would not survive, for they would be built on sand. A sensible man would not expect the sand to retain its position, but find out the winds which would remove it.[61]

The winds that removed the sand: he has noticed their strength, and the direction from which they blew in his own era. But have they always blown, and always from the same direction? A study of history would answer that question. The idea of testing his explanation for the failure of his ideal is first mentioned in a letter to Kergorlay in December 1850. A historian could do one of two things: either relate all the preceding facts, or select the facts which supported his explanation. His aim was to 'judge the facts, rather than to narrate them', the criterion for his judgement being 'that of liberty and human dignity'. [62]

It is perhaps odd that Tocqueville should even entertain the idea of finding permanent causes of human behaviour. The notion that all human history is determined by *de grandes causes premières* [great first causes] was repugnant to him, because he believed it excluded free choice. Indeed, he had often written down his objections to such theories—'narrow despite their pretensions to grandeur and false despite their air of mathematical truth'.[63] The objection is rounded off with a characteristic jibe—a tilt at the character and intellectual power of the men who indulge in these speculations, men who want to '*nourrir leur vanité*' [feed their vanity] or '*faciliter leur travail*' [lighten their labours]. And in the one history book which he published he is careful not to elevate the causes he mentions into 'great first causes' affecting the whole of human history. What he wanted to know was whether the causes he had cited for the failure of his ideal had operated in the past; and if so, what conclusions he could draw.

The study was not to extend beyond French history. What he planned was a survey of French history which would explain 'the nature of the institutions, the turn of mind, and the state of manners and morals'.[64] The first volume, *L'Ancien Régime et la Révolution*, was published in 1856. Unfortunately ill-health interrupted his work on the second and only a fragment of it was ready for publication at the time of his death. If Tocqueville had lived his three score years and ten (he was 54 when he died) we should undoubtedly have had a counterblast to Taine's *Les Origines de la France Contemporaine*. Surely Tocqueville's lamentations on the fate of liberty would be more tolerable than Taine's mob complex! But Tocqueville died, and the notes and sketches of the subsequent volumes are too incomplete to be of any service to the historian of France after 1789.

The curious thing is that in his quest for the causes of the failure of his ideal, he had incidentally written a great book on the origins of the French Revolution. We may well judge the talents of a historian by the questions he asks, and Tocqueville not only asks the right questions, but provides answers which have stood the test of time. In the introduction he formulates these questions: why did the Revolution break out in France and not in the other European countries; why did the Revolution 'issue, apparently spontaneously, from the society which it was destined to destroy' and why did the old monarchy fall so completely and so suddenly?[65] At the time discerning friends prophesied that all future historians would be indebted to his work.[66] This prophecy has been more than fulfilled. Even today the work is used as a text-book on the French Revolution, while research students working on the same period are still trying rather to patch up Tocqueville's conclusions in the light of fresh evidence than to present a completely new work on the origins of the Revolution. Oddly enough Taine, who owes so much to Tocqueville's pioneer work on the *Ancien Régime*, not only lacked the grace to acknowledge his debt to his distinguished predecessor, but even omitted to mention Tocqueville's book.

But the praise of others has been generous. Who could fail to admire the skill with which the facts are selected to support his ideas, the finesse with which the reader is led naturally from one reflection to another? As a man observing the flow of water towards a waterfall believes that the crash of the waters is the natural consequence of all that he has observed, so the reader believes that the crash of 1789 was the natural consequence of the preceding events. More: he knows what it felt like to be one of the members of that society. There was bitter hatred in that society, the hatred of the peasant for the nobles and the clergy. In a brief passage Tocqueville not only gives the explanation, but impresses the reasons indelibly on our minds: 'Whatever he (the peasant) may do, wherever he goes, he comes up against these troublesome neighbours who interfere with his pleasures, hamper his work and eat his produce. And when he has finished with these, others appear dressed in black, who take from him the pick of his crop. Just imagine the condition, the needs, the character, the passions of this man, and calculate, if you can, the accumulated hate and envy stored up in his heart'.[67] This is not an isolated example of his descriptive powers. These rich periods of language, the effective use of words—'these troublesome neighbours'—are sustained from the introduction to the conclusion. As a history book, the work deserves the respect and veneration accorded to it ever since its publication.

But these achievements were incidental. The main purpose was to find the reasons for man's indifference to liberty. The first test case which he planned to analyse was the *coup d'état* of Napoleon I: 'I shall endeavour to show by which events, mistakes and miscalculations these . . . Frenchmen came to abandon their foremost idea and, forgetful of liberty, no longer had any desire beyond becoming the equal servants of the master of the world',[68] who promptly deprived them of the main guarantee of liberty—the liberties. Unfortunately this task was never completed, but the first volume contains the answers to the key questions. The general outline is there; the second volume had only to fill in the details.

And what a familiar view! History confirms the opinions he had formed from personal observation. If anything it strengthens his conviction that liberty is unattainable so long as there is no restraint upon men's desire for material well-being. In history he sees the evidence of men's affection for equality, for the abolition of every privilege, and their envy of those with superior attainments. He sees too the relation between the movement towards equality and the creation of those institutions which were so inimical to liberty— administrative centralisation. Nor does a closer examination of this movement unsettle his first explanation for it. Once again belief in equality is explained as a 'taste', a permanent quality in human nature, while centralisation is explained away as one of the 'instincts' or the natural tendency of men with the taste for equality. He does not find any evidence that men have ever made liberty 'the primary good'. On the contrary, their attachment for it is so feeble that he doubts whether any but the very few will ever feel strongly for 'this sublime taste'. Only the 'great hearts', God's elect, are believers in liberty: 'One ought to give up hope of conveying its meaning to mediocre souls who have never been touched by it'.[69] This is the language of despair. History had confirmed the pessimistic conclusions formed from observation of his contemporaries.

The excursion into history and its fruits, pessimism and despair, provide a striking contrast to a similar performance by Marx. Like Tocqueville, he was disappointed with the results of the 1848 Revolution. He had hailed the fighting in the streets as the thunderclap heralding a new era. But instead, a nation of 36 millions was 'surprised and delivered unresisting into captivity by three high-class swindlers'.[70] Unlike Tocqueville, Marx is not inhibited by the opinions which plunged Tocqueville into despair. First, he demonstrates how the class struggle in France (not the 'depraved taste' or the 'natural tendency' or the indifference to the 'sublime taste') created circumstances and relationships which made it possible for a grotesque mediocrity to play a hero's part.[71] Then he turned to history to find the laws governing its development, and the result was a declaration of faith in man's power to build the good society, and a blue-print of the methods to be adopted to achieve that aim.

How different from Tocqueville! He too had a vision of a good society. Did it not float before his eyes whenever he reflected on the future of mankind? But reflection did not provide the means to achieve it. 'I gaze at it in a mournful, sad, distracted reverie which leads to nothing'.[72] Marx exhorted his contemporaries to speed up the advent of the new society—action would bring the day nearer. Tocqueville counsels resignation and renunciation of this world. Redemption will come not in this world but in the next. Alleviation of suffering, a reward for its noble endurance: men must not expect them in this world. These are the thoughts with which he consoles himself on the death of his uncle M. de Rosambo.

This desire to withdraw from the world affects his interests. Social and political questions almost disappear from his correspondence in the last three years of his life, while concern for personal salvation and interest in the mystery of life and death loom larger and larger as attachment to this world becomes more tenuous. The two most tangible signs of this withdrawal were the renewal of the religious practices which he had abandoned in adolescence, and his intimate friendship with the Christian mystic Madame Swetchine.[73]

True, he was a sick man, and the doctors could do little to relieve his pains. His disease—tuberculosis—was incurable. What he did not notice was that society, like himself, would be incurably sick if his diagnosis of its complaint—the undesirable qualities innate in man—was correct. Despair and withdrawal from human society were the logical consequences of his opinions on man. The man who began his public career with a message and a warning ended it in a minor key—death was a blessed relief.

We began this chapter with the simile used by Renan to illustrate the dilemma of French thinkers in the middle of the nineteenth century. The behaviour of Tocqueville and his reflections on the behaviour of his contemporaries may be usefully summarised by reverting to that simile. The pole in the centre of the flock represents the ideal by which he governed his conduct—at least he thought so until the behaviour of one section of the flock, the socialists, stimulated a desire to escape from the restricted area defined by the pole. This was our first conclusion: his attachment to his ideal weakened when the use of its instruments, the liberties, threatened his personal creed. And the second was almost a corollary to the first: the pole defined the pasture for the sheep—if we were restricted to such a confined space, we should be powerless to deal with conditions in society which disturbed our conscience. And the third was equally depressing: to accept Tocqueville we must believe that even if we had the opportunity to graze in fresh pastures, we should not have the power to enjoy them rightly, for no matter how good the intention, our behaviour was determined by qualities in our nature which could not be subdued without the aid of a 'higher discipline'. Here then were the three responses to the test: modification when circumstances demand it; a clarification of the type of society favourable to the ideal; a confession that the ideal is unattainable unless the nature of man changes. Is it worth while to pursue an ideal with such a poor record? We shall attempt to answer this question in the fifth and concluding chapter of this work.

## Endnotes

[1] R. W. Postgate: *Revolution from 1789–1806*, p. 169.
[2] Ibid., pp. 199–201.
[3] Ibid., pp. 106–7.

4   'J'ai toujours jugé que les institutions démocratiques et républicaines étaient l'avenir de la France'. Circular to electors of Valognes (in archives at Tocqueville).

5   See his letter to E. Stoffels given in footnote on pp. 79–80.

6   'Je demande sans cesse les noms de ces inconnus que je vois tous les jours'. *Souvenirs*, p. 123.

7   Ibid.

8   'C'est nous qui mangerons les ailes de poulet!' Ibid., p. 219.

9   'la révolution de 1789 est sortie du cerveau et du coeur de la nation; mais celle-ci a pris en partie naissance dans son estomac'. *OE. C.* VII, 235–6: Letter to M. Bouchitté, Paris, 1.5.1848.

10   'un homme dont le souvenir m'a toujours rempli de dégoût et d'horreur'. *Souvenirs*, p. 181.

11   Ibid., p. 206.

12   'ce qu'on appelle les institutions nécessaires ne sont souvent que les institutions aux-quelles on est accoutumé, et qu'en matière de constitution sociale, le champ du possible est bien plus vaste que les hommes qui vivent dans chaque société ne se l'imaginent.' Ibid., p. 111.

13   'la liberté est perdue sans ressource'. Ibid., p. 94.

14   'Je me décidai à me jeter à corps perdu dans l'arène, et à risquer pour la defense, non pas de tel gouvernement, mais des lois qui constituent la société même, ma fortune, mon repos et ma personne.' Ibid., p. 126.

15   K. Marx: *The Class Struggles in France*, p. 47.

16   'l'action désordonnée des masses, leur intervention violente et mal éclairée dans les affaires'. A. Rédier: op. cit., p. 48.

17   'se répandre du côté ou penche le verre', *OE. C.* IX, 131–2. Speech to the 'Académie des Sciences Morales et Politiques', 5.4.1852.

18   'Je ne doute pas que les lois constitutifs de notre société moderne ne soient fort modifiés à la longue', *Souvenirs*, p. 111.

19   Ibid., p. 340.

20   'le seul moyen qui restait après une si violente révolution de sauver la liberté était de la restreindre'. Ibid.

21   J. P. Mayer, op. cit., p. 73.

22   Ibid., p. 75.

23   Jellinek, op. cit., p. 130.

24   W. Bagehot: *Literary Studies*, vol. I: Appendix I, p. 277.

25   'malentendu terrible entre les classes'. K. Marx: *The Class Struggles in France*, pp. 44–5.

26   R. W. Postgate, op. cit., p. 215.

27   Normanby: *A Year of Revolution from a journal kept in Paris in 1848*, vol. II, p. 17. A detailed account of this incident is given in Garnier-Pagès: *Histoire de la Révol-ution de 1848*, vol. XI, pp. 356–64.

28   Ibid., II, 101.

29   *Souvenirs*, pp. 109–10.

30   'l'objet le plus sérieux que les philosophes et les hommes d'Etat puissent regarder'. Ibid., p. 111.

31   *OE. C.* IX, 539.

32   Ibid.

33   'de choses plus hautes et plus belles, c'est en parlant de la patrie … de vertu, de générosité, de désintéressement, de gloire qu'elle a fait de grandes choses'. Ibid., 541–2.

[34] *'Dans l'avenir personne ne tuera personne, la terre rayonnera, le genre humain aimera. Il viendra, citoyens, ce jour ou tout sera concorde, harmonie, lumière, joie et vie, il viendra. Et c'est pour qu'il vienne que nous allons mourir.'* V. Hugo: *Les Misérables*, III, 463.

[35] R. W. Postgate, op. cit., p. 215.

[36] *OE. C.* IX, 540. Speech to the Constituent Assembly, 12.9.1848.

[37] Ibid.

[38] *'Marques très vives d'assentiment'.* Ibid.

[39] *'les différents formes qu'a prises … quoiqu'on dise, le droit de propriété sur la terre'.* *Souvenirs*, p. 111.

[40] *'défiance profonde de la liberté'. OE. C.* IX, 540, v.s.

[41] *'étend la sphère de l'indépendance individuelle'* but socialism *'la resserre'.* Ibid., 546.

[42] *'doit se placer autour de lui, pour le guider, le garantir, le maintenir, le retenir'.* Ibid., 541.

[43] Ibid., 544.

[44] Ibid., 551.

[45] K. Marx: *The Class Struggles in France*, p. 143.

[46] K. Marx: *The 19th Brumaire of Louis Bonaparte*, p. 57.

[47] Ibid., p. 100.

[48] Ibid.

[49] *Souvenirs*, p. 115.

[50] J. P. Mayer, op. cit., pp. 85–6.

[51] M. C. M. Simpson: *Correspondence and Conversations of A. de Tocqueville with Nassau William Senior from 1834 to 1859*, II, p. 7.

[52] Ibid., II, p. 4.

[53] Unpublished letter in archives at Tocqueville, written to Beaumont, at Tocqueville, 23.3.1853.

[54] M. C. M. Simpson: op. cit., I, p. 271.

[55] *'Je serais bien fâché d'être moins triste … car je suis triste à mourir'.* Unpublished letter in archives at Tocqueville, written to Beaumont, at Tocqueville, 13.1.1852.

[56] M. C. M. Simpson: op. cit., II, 22.

[57] Unpublished letter in archives at Tocqueville, written to Beaumont, at Tocqueville, 22.4.1852.

[58] *'ils n'attachent plus de prix aux biens auxquels tout mon coeur est resté lié'. OE.C.* VI, 350. Letter to Mme Swetchine, Tocqueville, 20.10.1856.

[59] Ibid., 351.

[60] *'On pourrait croire qu'il n'y a jamais eu d'institutions libres en France, â voir l'étonnement qu'on inspire quand on en parle aux gens'.* Unpublished letter in archives at Tocqueville, 22.4.1852.

[61] Ibid.

[62] *'juger les faits plutôt qu'à les raconter'; 'celle de la liberté et de la dignité humaine'. OE.C.* VII, 257–264. Letter to Kergorlay, Sorrento, 15.12.1850.

[63] *'étroits dans leur prétendue grandeur, et faux sous leur air de vérité mathématique'. Souvenirs*, pp. 88–9.

[64] *'la nature des institutions, le tour des esprits, l'état des mœurs'.* Ibid.

[65] *est sortie comme d'elle même de la société qu'elle allait détruire'. L'Ancien Régime. Avant-Propos.*

[66] Unpublished letter at Tocqueville. Letter from Sir G. C. Lewis to Tocqueville, 3.9.1856.

67 'Quoi qu'il fasse, il rencontre partout sur son chemin ces voisins incommodes, pour troubler son plaisir, gêner son travail, manger ses produits; et quand il a fini avec ceux-ci, d'autres, vêtus de noir, se présentent, qui lui prennent le plus clair de sa récolte. Figurez-vous la condition, les besoins, le caractère, les passions de cet homme, et calculez si vous le pouvez, les trésors de haine et d'envie qui se sont ramassés dans son coeur'. *L'Ancien Régime*, 46.

68 'je tâcherai de montrer par quelles événements, quelles fautes, quels mécomptes, ces . . . Français sont arrivés à abandonner leur première idée, et oubliant la liberté, n'ont plus voulu que devenir les serviteurs égaux du maître du monde'. Ibid., vii.

69 'on doit renoncer à le faire comprendre aux âmes médiocres qui ne l'ont jamais ressenti'. Ibid., 248.

70 K. Marx: *The 18th Brumaire of Louis Bonaparte*, p. 18.

71 Ibid., p. 8.

72 'Je suis en face de lui dans une contemplation morne, triste, et distraite, qui ne mène à rien'. *OE.C.* VII, 299: Letter to Bouchitté, Saint-Cyr, 23.9.1853.

73 A. Rédier, op. cit., p. 282.

# Chapter V
## Conclusion

To ridicule an idea when sincerely held is said to be an offence against the canons of good taste. To debunk it is evidence either of the author's arrogance or of crude indifference to the wounded sensibilities of the believers. Correct conduct in criticism is a strait-jacket shackling the mind, or rather, the critic who observes these standards is like a horse with blinkers—aware of the objective to which the idealist would lead him, but ignorant of the pitfalls and dangers which beset him on every side. No wonder the men who break free from the strait-jacket, or tear the blinkers from their eyes, are vituperative and fierce in their criticism of the restraints which held them in bondage. The strongest and most determined opponents of religion are generally the men who were formerly devout believers: the strength of the opposition is equal to the strength of the belief.

Evaluation of Tocqueville's ideal depends on the type of blinkers the critic wears. If they permit us to see the vision which floated before his eyes—men doing what is good and just without compulsion—and the grace and charm, the exquisite behaviour of those who pursue this ideal, we may be tempted to join this tiny band on their pilgrimage to the Elysian fields. After all, sympathy with Tocqueville is a sign of superior qualities: only the 'great hearts' understood his aims. And if the way was hard, the road beset with quagmires, that was not the fault of the travellers, but of the 'mediocre individuals' who, in their zest for earthly pleasures, had torn up the road along which his pilgrims must pass in their passage from one eternity to another. But if we remove the blinkers which Tocqueville asks us to wear, and observe the path we are asked to follow with open eyes, we shall be alarmed by the poor equipment of our fellow travellers, shocked by the means we have to use to cross the quagmires, and disgusted by the conditions in which many of us would be obliged to live at the end of our journey, if we scrupulously observe his ideal. To be uncritical on such a journey, to maintain an air of respect and reverence would be to acquiesce in a great evil, or, like Tocqueville, to be so distressed by the obstacles that despair and resignation become the only sensible attitude to life.

For the first and most striking characteristic of those liberals, who bemused their contemporaries with their dream of harmony, is the tension between mind and heart. With his mind Tocqueville assented to the notion of equality. The behaviour of a 'master' to his 'servant' was obsolete, and unbecoming in a society which had abandoned privilege. Even the crude manners and ways of life of the Americans must be tolerated as the concomitant of equality, though the refined may nurse the hope that their manners may be purified. But the objections of the heart to this ideal cannot be silenced by even the most rigorous discipline. As we saw in the chapter on 'Man and Ideal', the conversion to democratic ways of life was an intellectual one: it did not affect his own behaviour or his personal attitude to the middle and lower classes. The man who urged his contemporaries to accept equality was not a very faithful adherent to the ideal. Close contact with the working classes always stimulated loathing and contempt, and sometimes fear. The contempt was harmless provided he expressed it in circles in sympathy with his own reaction. But the fear was disastrous to the realisation of his ideal.

For equality entailed association with working men, which in his case always concluded with the decision to defend a way of life inimical to the pursuit of his ideal. In 1830 he was stunned and horrified by what he saw, but at that time he was not a believer in democracy. In 1848 he decided to risk 'my fortune, my security, and my life', while in the years between these two revolutions, the one fear which haunts his mind is the possible recurrence of the 'disturbances'.

Here is the paradox in the life of liberals like Tocqueville: on the one hand, the ideal of the good society, but on the other hand, disgust with the sordidness of its birth—a disgust which developed into a terror whenever working men chose the barricade rather than the Chamber to realise their demands. We have seen that Tocqueville was by no means unique in his attitude to the masses. All the members of his class—the refined intellectuals—were alarmed by the avalanche which overwhelmed them in 1848. We have noticed the reactions of Guizot and Proudhon. Even Lamartine, the apostle of fraternity and the leader of the February revolution, had only an intellectual attachment to the idea of equality: 'my heart is with the party of that forgotten generation, whereas my mind is with the party of the future'.[1] But social change could be realised only with the support of the masses and the masses meant, in practice, civil disorder, violence, savagery—and this terrified the refined intellectuals. So Lamartine, like Tocqueville, Guizot and Proudhon, discovered by May of 1848 that there was a greater good than the ideal of the *'parti de l'avenir'* [party of the future]—order—and to preserve it he was prepared to sacrifice his life.[2] The interesting point is that his heart was with *'cette génération oubliée* [that forgotten generation]. He, too, became a renegade in the presence of the masses. It would, of course, be callous to ridicule the fears of these liberals, or to accuse them of fleeing before a hallucination. They were the descendants of the families who had suffered persecution, loss of property, emigration, even death during the French Revolution; they were educated by men and women who were dependent on their class for their existence. Even 1830, if less violent than its illustrious predecessor, was a rude reminder that their class might be liquidated by the masses. Indeed, as late as 1837, hatred and suspicion of the aristocracy were still so strong that Tocqueville attributed his failure to be elected [to the Chamber of Deputies] to his association with that class. Again, all his election speeches begin with a repudiation of the values of his class.* Did not Guizot declare that the vital issue in French politics was whether one died with one's head under the guillotine or on the pillow? And was not Tocqueville himself angered by the anxiety of his contemporaries for order? The more familiar we become with their experience and the more we learn of the 'stories' told to them in childhood (and the picture of the world formed in childhood is rarely erased from the mind), the more intelligible their attitude to the masses becomes. We may believe that the participation of the masses in politics does not mean 'murder, arson and savagery'³ but refined intellectuals such as Tocqueville and Lamartine did. And so long as they were under the influence of this idea, the ideals which they preached were abandoned as soon as the terror seized them.

Here then is the first conclusion: to know the ideals and behaviour which Tocqueville and other liberals approved of, observe not only what they say in the salon or write in the study when the 'cool head' works uninhibited by the 'burning passions', but observe also their behaviour in the streets, in the Chamber, indeed wherever the atmosphere is uncongenial. In all the crucial tests their attachment to their ideals is too slight to stand the strain. To read Tocqueville, to read the works of any comparable idealist, is in some ways like listening to a Beethoven quartet: it exalts and ennobles the mind. But alas, this exaltation may be deceptive. Its effect may be only

---

* One example of this is his speech to the electors of Valognes of the 13th February 1839:

On vous dira encore qu'appartenant à une famille ancienne je veux ramener la société aux anciens préjugés, aux anciens privilèges, aux anciens usages; ce sont encore là non seulement des calomnies odieuses, mais ridicules. Il n'y a pas en France et je ne crains pas de le dire, en Europe, un seul homme qui ait fait voir d'une manière plus publique qu l'ancienne société aristocratique avait disparu pour toujours, et qu'il ne restait plus aux hommes de notre temps qu'à organiser progressivement et prudemment sur ses ruines la société démocratique nouvelle.

[You will also be told that, belonging to an old family, I want to lead society back to the old prejudices, the old privileges and the old customs. These calumnies are not only odious, but ridiculous. There is not a single man in France, in fact I make bold to say, in Europe, who has shown in a more public manner that the old aristocratic society has disappeared forever and that it only remains for the men of our time to organise the new democratic society, progressively and prudently, on its ruins.] (*OE. C.* IX, 224).

temporary, or it may have no effect on behaviour.[1] The Russian nobles at the end of the eighteenth century were exalted by the lofty sentiments expressed in the works of *les Philosophes*. But this did not prevent these readers from inflicting cruel punishments on their house servants and serfs—in some cases 500 strokes with the rod for failure to attend Holy Communion—and this, sometimes, at the command of a master who was enjoying Voltaire's satire on the Church!

Not that Tocqueville himself was guilty of such an extreme discrepancy between his ideals and his behaviour. On the contrary, he was humane and revolted by cruelty, though his remoteness from every-day things often obscured the suffering and the misery of his contemporaries. It is not lack of sympathy which estranges the liberals from the masses. The pages of European literature in the nineteenth century are filled with penitent noblemen, who renounce their wordly possessions and preach the doctrine of fraternity to hearts hardened by years of servitude and physical suffering. This gesture, however, was not the fashion in Tocqueville's generation. In his generation the conscientious preached ideals. But the vision of harmony vanished as soon as the bogey of the masses intruded on their consciousness.

To put it bluntly: their ideal could not withstand the shock of one unpleasant experience. Yet it is the Tocquevilles, the Lamartines and the Proudhons who exhort men to pursue the good life, to govern their conduct by lofty ideals. And it is men of similar temperament and social background but without their intellectual powers who are responsive to this kind of appeal. They are the class who appreciate their books, applaud their speeches and rejoice when their teachers, too, wilt before the 'dirty collar', the coarse, crude lower orders with their vulgar appetites and their petty pleasures. If society depended on the armchair converts to equality and fraternity for the creation of the good society, the men who bore the burden of economic inequality would have to be contented with

---

[1] On p. 125 of the copy text, Clark inserts the sentence, now included in the text, which begins 'Its effect may be only temporary . . .'. He removes the following sentence: 'Hitler, we are told, also weeps when he listens to music'.

the promise of such a society. Tocqueville's intentions were good; his actions were inhibited by strong and overwhelming emotions. The radical sentiments of an idealist of his type are as chaff before the wind: only the roots will weather the storm, and the roots are deeply embedded in the past, in the 'party of that forgotten generation', and not the 'party of the future'.

The second characteristic of men such as Tocqueville is their belief that the spiritual pleasures are superior to the material, that the pleasures derived from the things of the mind are of a higher order than the pleasures derived from material comfort, the satisfaction of the appetites. The objection we make to this position is not the evaluation but the attitude adopted towards those who insist that men must first be provided with earthly bread before they can enjoy heavenly bread. With Tocqueville, as indeed with all idealists, the important thing is the state of men's minds, and they are reluctant to admit that the opinions which men hold are influenced by their environment. When they notice that the poor accept the socialist thesis that the good state of mind depends on a full stomach and a comfortable home, they become disgusted with their values, accuse them of materialism, of pandering to the lower passions and strive to rid their minds of these dangerous opinions. The Mayor's retort to the priest in Ibsen's *Brand*—

> It was not words I bade you share
> They're barren when the belly's bare[4]

—is, unfortunately, only persuasive to those who accept the argument that men will be more likely to do what is good and just when their material needs are satisfied. To a Tocqueville, or any man with the same values, such a remark would be not only shocking but evidence of a depraved mind.

And yet so long as men accept his position, the economic equality which he postulated as an essential condition for the pursuit of his ideal is unattainable. What is more serious: the men whose motives for opposing the socialists are not so 'lofty' as his, will be able to use his arguments to preserve the status quo. In discussing his reactions to 1848, we saw how disgusted he was by the behaviour and values of those who proposed to build a new heaven on earth. But the only effective opposition to the socialists was organised by men whose motives were equally materialist. The cynics may sneer at the mental gymnastics he performed during those critical years to reconcile his behaviour with his ideal. At least Tocqueville had the honesty and courage to denounce Louis Napoleon's solution—the use of compulsion to suppress the socialists. But courage and loyalty to ideals alone will not create that material well-being which he himself confessed was indispensable for the realisation of his ideal, although he objected so strongly to making it the main objective of political action. Unless men accept the principle that material well-being is the sine qua non of the good society, all attempts to realise his ideal will be vitiated by recurring class conflict. It is difficult to see how material well-being for all men can be achieved as long as the power of the state is limited as Tocqueville directed.

But even if he had changed his opinion on the importance of material well-being, we doubt whether men would do what is good and just <u>without compulsion</u>. Tocqueville's idea was that if men had religious beliefs, they would both know what was good and do it. But the difficulty with this position is that there is no agreement on the definition of the 'good'—that religious beliefs are often, to the believer, a strong recommendation and support for the behaviour and opinions of which he personally approves. In fact a man may claim divine support for opinions which are antithetical to Tocqueville's ideal. Indeed, he may claim that he reached these opinions by the use of that free-will (*libre arbitre*) which Tocqueville maintained was God's greatest gift to mankind. In such a contingency, a faithful observance of his ideal is disastrous to the behaviour and opinions which he is recommending to his fellow-men. Men will use the liberties to persuade others to accept a régime which is hostile to his values. This happened in December 1851. In the period from 1918–39 it happened so frequently that men faithful to the liberal creed despaired of finding a deterrent. This is perhaps the most crucial problem for the believer in liberty: to find an effective deterrent to the opinions and behaviour which vitiate their ideal without using compulsion. We have stated our objections to Tocqueville's deterrent—religious beliefs. If there is no effective deterrent except compulsion, to refuse to use it is to find ourselves, like Prometheus, bound to the beetling crags while the vultures—in Tocqueville's time the Bonapartists, in ours the Fascists—exploit our helplessness, use the facilities we provide for them, and then administer the *coup de grâce* to the exhausted defenders of the liberal creed.

Here then are the fundamental objections to the ideal of Alexis de Tocqueville: that he was not prepared to accept the social and political changes required if all were to pursue his ideal; that he was too detached from the life of the masses to perceive that the behaviour he disapproved of was more the effect of poverty than of a depraved mind, that for the great mass of mankind earthly bread is essential for happiness and peace of mind; most important, that he never found an effective guarantee that men would do what was good and just without compulsion. What I have tried to stress is the consequences of excluding compulsion. It prevents action against two great problems in our society: poverty and the use of the 'liberties' to establish a Fascist dictatorship.[m]

It is perhaps easy to indicate the objections to Tocqueville's ideal, but it requires hard and bitter mental labour to suggest an alternative. The modern commentaries on the liberals peter out with the reader convinced of the futility of the liberal creed, but uninformed or unimpressed by the suggestions given for future action. I too feel the temptation, as it were, to lower the curtain with the hero of the drama extinct and a chorus of voices lamenting the fate of human beings who have a vision of the good life, but are deprived of its enjoyment by a malignant fate or by the viciousness of human nature. But resignation and renunciation were the final

---

[m]  On p. 130 of the copy text, Clark inserts the sentence, now included in the text, which begins: 'What I have tried to stress . . .'. He removes the following sentences: 'What we have tried to stress throughout is the consequences of a faithful observance of the methods which he postulated—the continuation of poverty and the inability to prevent the contrary to his ideal, the Bonapartist régime or a Fascist dictatorship. And it is because I believe that the consequences were not fortuitous either in his time or in ours that I maintain that to avoid them we must abandon his ideal'.

position of Tocqueville and we have assumed that this is not a desirable attitude to human events. What then is to be done? Are we to assume that men will never do what is good and just? If we examine Tocqueville's definition of his ideal, the words which create the difficulties are 'liberty' and 'without compulsion'. Indeed, I believe that the first move we must make is to scrap this liberal definition of the good life and ask two questions: what is the good society, and how is it to be realised?

And, of course, as soon as we pose the first question, we raise the difficulty which confronted Tocqueville. The conception of the good society varies from man to man. For some it is a society in which the principle 'From each according to his ability, to each according to his needs' is observed; for others it is a society in which the incentive to work is the service of Christ: 'Inasmuch as ye did it unto the least of my children ye did it unto me'. But even if the majority agreed to accept a society organised on either of these principles (in parenthesis I should point out that there is no reason why there should be any difference in the <u>organisation</u> if some worked for human reasons while others worked for divine) there would still be the difficulty of persuading the minority to co-operate. And, at the moment, the main difficulty is that only the minority accept either of these ideals as the fundamental principles of human association. So this minority must either have faith in the justice of their ideal, and believe that it is possible to 'convert' the majority to its position by education, or, as with the Communists, so organise their supporters that it is possible to destroy the old society by force and rely on the attractions of the new society to convert the opposition, the assumption being that the gains will outweigh the price paid.*

For those who believe that this is too high a price to pay for human harmony, the determination of the Communists to repeat

---

* This was the argument which Lenin used to Gorky to justify the cruelty and violence against the members of the old society in Russia: 'Our generation achieved something of amazing significance for history. The cruelty, which the conditions of our life made necessary, will be understood and vindicated. Everything will be understood!' (M. Gorky: *Days with Lenin*, Current Book Distributors edition, p. 27)

these methods in other countries if necessary, should spur them to intensify their efforts to convert the rest by more humane methods. But what of the minority who refuse to conform or who use their liberties to destroy the good society? Let us be brutally frank: they must be compelled to conform, or if this is too repellent to the leaders of the new society, they must be prevented from influencing other members of society. This may mean imprisonment or exile, or, at least, a prohibition on their right to express their opinions in public either in speech or writing. What is, I think, certain is that the authorities must not be prevented from acting by such scruples as 'no compulsion'. The fatal helplessness of the liberal ideal must be avoided. It should not be beyond the power of man to devise deterrents and prohibitions which would effectively suppress the 'toughs' without shocking the sensibilities of the men of good will.

This then is the task of the men who retain their faith in the future of mankind: to convert others to this ideal, and to devise humane methods to suppress the opposition. But the first task is to convince those who are still under the spell of the great liberals of the past century that their ideal is more a hindrance than a help. The best antidote to their influence is to study the personal fate of one of the finest representatives of this school—Alexis de Tocqueville. True, some may use his experience to prove with Plato that 'no human affairs are worth taking very seriously',[5] or with Christ that in this world there will always be tribulation,[6] or with the Chinese philosopher Tao Te Ching that 'it is better to say nothing and to hold fast to the mean between too much and too little confidence in heaven and earth'.[7] Perhaps it depends on the mood of the moment. But resignation is not an incentive to action, and, in the meantime, the evils which prompted these reflections continue. We may draw inspiration from the advice of another man of goodwill, Pericles: 'The strongest-hearted are those who with the clearest vision of both the pleasant and the unpleasant things in a situation do not shrink from facing it'.[8] A study of Tocqueville gives just this clear vision of things pleasant and unpleasant, both the reasons for resignation and the vision of what must be done if we are to avoid the pessimism of his last years as a member of human society.

## Endnotes

[1] '*Mon cœur est du parti de cette génération oubliée, bien que mon intelligence soit du parti de l'avenir*'. A. de Lamartine, 'Le Drapeau Rouge' printed in *Lectures pour Tous*, p. 510.

[2] Ibid.

[3] '*des meurtres, des incendies, et la sauvagerie*'. H. Taine, *La Révolution*, I, p. 407.

[4] H. Ibsen: *Brand* (Heinemann edition, London, 1912), p. 40.

[5] Plato: *The Republic* (Everyman edition), p. 307.

[6] St John's Gospel, chapter 16, verse 33.

[7] *Chinese Philosophy in Classical Times* (Everyman edition), p. 147.

[8] Quoted in L. Woolf; *The Barbarians at the Gate*, p. 78. [From *Thucydides*, Book II.]

# APPENDIX I
## Life of Tocqueville

| | |
|---|---|
| **1805** | Born at Paris. Father was Comte de Tocqueville; mother was daughter of Le Peletier de Rosanbo; maternal great-grandfather was Monsieur de Malesherbes. Christened Alexis-Charles-Henri-Clérel de Tocqueville. |
| **1817–23** | Studied at Metz. He was awarded first prize for rhetoric in 1822, but was considered a poor student of Latin and Greek. His father was prefect at Metz. |
| **1824–5** | Studied Law in Paris. |
| **1825** | Wrote article attacking democracy. |
| **1826** | Visited Italy and Sicily with his brother Edouard. |
| **1827** | Recalled by Royal ordinance and made *juge auditeur* at Versailles tribunal. |
| **1830** | Appointed *juge adjoint*. |
| **1831** | Tocqueville and Beaumont left for America to study penitentiary system. |
| **1832** | Resigned from position as *juge adjoint* as protest against the dismissal of Beaumont. |
| **1832** | Published with Beaumont *Du Système Pénitentiaire*. |
| **1832–4** | Wrote first two volumes of *De la Démocratie en Amérique*. |
| **1835** | Published *De la Démocratie en Amérique*, Part I. |
| **1835** | Second visit to England. Married Miss Marie Mottley in October. |
| **1836** | Travelled in Switzerland. |

Awarded prize by *Académie Française* for *De la Démocratie en Amérique*, Part I.

1836      Failed in candidature for *Arrondissement* of Valognes for the Chamber of Deputies.

1838      Elected member of the *Académie des Sciences morales et politiques.*

1839      Elected to the Chamber of Deputies by electors of Valognes, and retained the seat at every subsequent election which he contested.

1840      Publication of *De la Démocratie en Amérique*, Part II. For the next 12 years literary activity is replaced by political activity.

1841      Visited Algeria.

Elected member of the French Academy.

1843      Elected to *Conseil Général de la Manche.*

1846      Report on Algeria, defining the principles of colonisation.

1847      3 July—Refused invitation to attend reform banquets.

October—Published *De la Classe Moyenne et du Peuple.*

1848      27 January—Speech to Assembly prophesying the Revolution.

October—Chosen to represent France at Brussels Conference called for intervention by England and France in dispute between Austria and Sardinia.

1849      1 June—Re-elected to Legislative Assembly and became Vice-President of the Assembly.

2 June—Appointed Foreign Minister under Barrot.

31 October—Presidential message, after which Barrot ministry resigned.

1850      Wrote *Souvenirs* Part I at Tocqueville.

**December 1850 to March 1851** Wrote *Souvenirs* Part II at Sorrento.

1851      9 July—Report to Constituent Assembly on the influence of Centralisation in France.

2 December—Returned to Paris, attended meeting of 10th Arrondissement, signed resolution condemning *coup d'état*, was taken with 200 others to the *caserne du quai d'Orsay* and that night transferred to Vincennes. End of political life. Was immediately released and retired to Normandy.

11 December—Letter to the Editor of the *Times* protesting against Napoleon III's *coup d'état*.

**1854**     Research for his work on *Ancien Régime*, studied ancient provincial administrations, especially in Tours, at Saint-Cyr.

**1855**     Travelled in Germany to study feudal structure of society.

**1856**     Publication of *L'Ancien Régime et la Révolution* Part I.

**1857**     May to June—In England, engaged in research on material for Part II of *L'Ancien Régime et la Révolution*. Read confidential correspondence of English government with its diplomatic agents on the continent. On his return to France, the First Lord of the Admiralty provided a special boat for the Channel crossing.

**1859**     16 April—Died at Cannes.

# BIBLIOGRAPHY

## A. Introductory note

The first edition of the *Oeuvres Complètes* was published by G. de Beaumont in 1868. Unfortunately for students of Tocqueville, Beaumont had to satisfy three exacting censors—Napoleon III's government, his own personal opinions and the wishes of the Tocqueville family. The criticism of Napoleon III in *Souvenirs* was too severe to permit publication, while the scathing references to the French royal family were too offensive to the royalist sympathies of his own family. So Beaumont did not include *Souvenirs* in the *Oeuvres Complètes*. When they were finally published by the Comte de Tocqueville in 1893, the references to the French royal family were toned down. Beaumont also omitted the intimate correspondence with Tocqueville's wife, Marie Mottley, a correspondence which is a valuable source of knowledge of Tocqueville's character and beliefs. In 1937 the present Comte de Tocqueville authorised A. Rédier to prepare a new edition of the works. Rédier and his collaborators, L. Monnier and J. P. Mayer, were working on this edition when the war interrupted their work. My own judgements on Tocqueville are based on the material in the *Oeuvres Complètes* and *Souvenirs*, plus the unpublished letters and notebooks which I read during my stay at Tocqueville.

## B. Beaumont's Edition

*Oeuvres Complètes d'Alexis de Tocqueville* publiées par Me. Tocqueville (IX tomes Paris 1868).

I–III   *De la Démocratie en Amérique* (The text used is that of the 13th edition, see below).

IV   *L'Ancien Régime et la Révolution*.

V–VII  *Correspondence.*
 VIII  *Mélanges.*
  IX  *Etudes.*

## C.  Unpublished Material at Tocqueville

There were in 1939 ninety-five large folders of manuscript in the tower of the Château of Tocqueville. This unpublished material would probably fill four times as many volumes as that included in Beaumont's edition. The most important writings omitted by Beaumont are:

1. The correspondence with Marie de Tocqueville (his wife).
2. The text of *Souvenirs.*
3. Notes on 'Liberté d'Enseignement'.
4. Material on his political activity in the electorate of Valognes.
5. *Notes d'Amérique*, the diary of his American journey. A selection from these was published in Volume VIII of the *Oeuvres Complètes.*
6. *Ouvrage sur l'Inde*, an uncompleted work.

## D.  Separate Publications

1. *Du Système Pénitentiaire aux Etats-Unis.* 1st edition Paris 1833, 2nd edition Paris 1836, 3rd edition Paris 1845. (In collaboration with G. de Beaumont: not in the *OE.C.*)
2. 'Etat Social et Politique de la France avant et depuis 1789', first published in the *London and Westminster Review*, 1836. Translated and published by H. Reeve in 1856 with reprints in 1873 and 1888. (Included by Beaumont in Tome VIII of the *OE.C.*)
3. *De la Démocratie en Amérique* (Tomes I–III in the *OE.C.*)
   a. *De la Démocratie en Amérique*, part 1, Paris 1835. 5th edition Paris 1836 includes Tocqueville's revisions.
   b. *De la Démocratie en Amérique*, part 2, Paris 1840.
   c. *De la Démocratie en Amérique 13e édition . . . corrigée et augmentée d'un examen comparatif de la Démocratie aux Etats-Unis et en Suisse et d'un appendice*, 2 tomes, Paris 1850.

In English:
   d. *Democracy in America*: translated by H. Reeve. 4 vols. London 1838–40. 1840 new edition. 1875 new edition includes a biographical notice by the translator and some additional notes.
   e. *Democracy in America* (selections from Tocqueville with comments) by J. C. Spicer, New York 1851.
   f. *American Institutions of A. de Tocqueville*, revised and edited with notes by F. Bowen, Boston 1870.

4. *Souvenirs* (not in the *O.E.C.*)
    a. *Souvenirs d'Alexis de Tocqueville*, published by the Comte de Tocqueville, Paris 1893.
    b. *The Recollections of Alexis de Tocqueville*. Edited by the Comte de Tocqueville, and now first translated into English by A. T. Mattos. With a portrait. London 1896.
5. *L'Ancien Régime et la Révolution* (Tome IV of the *O.E.C.*)
    a. *L'Ancien Régime et la Révolution*, Paris 1856. 4th edition 1860 (this includes minor revisions by Tocqueville and is the edition used for modern French and English texts).
    b. *De Tocqueville's L'Ancien Régime*, edited with introduction and notes by G. W. Headlam, Oxford 1904.
    c. *L'Ancien Régime* translated by M. W. Patterson, Oxford 1933.
6. *Quinze Jours au Désert et Voyage en Sicile*. Edited by Jean Edmund Mannin. Oxford 1904 (Oxford Modern French Series, edited by Jean Delbos).

## E.  Works containing Speeches, Conversations or Correspondence by Tocqueville

1. *Parliamentary Papers*, June 1835. Minutes of evidence taken before the select committee on bribery at elections, on 22nd June 1835. Sir R. Peel quoted Tocqueville.
2. *Correspondence entre Alexis de Tocqueville et Arthur de Gobineau, 1843–59*, edited by L. Schemann, Paris 1909.
3. *Memoirs of Life and Correspondence of H. Reeve* by J. Laughton, London 1898. (This work contains reports of conversations between Reeve and Tocqueville.)
4. *Memoirs, letters and remains of Alexis de Tocqueville*. Translated from the French. 2 vols, Cambridge 1861. (The material used in this edition was included by Beaumont in vols V and VI of the *O.E.C.*)
5. *Madame Swetchine, sa Vie et ses Oeuvres*, par M. de Falloux, 2 tomes, Paris 1872. (This work contains some letters written by Tocqueville to Mme Swetchine which were not published in the *O.E.C.*)
6. *Correspondence and Conversation of Alexis de Tocqueville with Nassau William Senior, 1836–59*, edited by M. C. M. Simpson, 2 vols, London 1872. (Very useful for Tocqueville's reactions to 1848–52).

## F.  Opinions on Tocqueville

This list is not exhaustive. It was compiled from the catalogues of the Bodleian Library and the British Museum, and the reviews collected by the Tocqueville family and preserved in the archives at Tocqueville.

**a) 1835–69**

1. Reviews of *De la Démocratie en Amérique*. An exhaustive list is published in Pierson's work. Below we mention the most important.

   a. Léon Faucher: 'De la Démocratie aux Etats-Unis', in *Le Courier Français*, 1843 and 1841.

   b. F. de Corcille: 'De la Démocratie Américaine', in the *Revue des Deux Mondes*, 1853.

   c. J. S. Mill: Review of first part of *De la Démocratie en Amérique* in the *London Review*, 1835, also in the *Monthly Review* in 1835.

   d. Lockhart: Review of first part of *De la Démocratie en Amérique* in *Quarterly Review*, 1836.

   e. Villemain: Review of second part of *De la Démocratie en Amérique* in the *Journal des Savants*, 1840.

   f. J. S. Mill: *Democracy in America*, in *Edinburgh Review*, 1840. (Republished in Vol. II of J. S. Mill's *Dissertations and Discussions*, 3 vols, London 1867.)

   g. Rossi: Review of second part of *De la Démocratie en Amérique*, in *Revue des Deux Mondes*, 1840.

2. Reviews of *L'Ancien Régime et la Révolution*. (An exhaustive list of these is being prepared by J. P. Mayer.)

   a. Rossi: In *Revue des Deux Mondes*, 1856.

3. Obituary Notices.

   a. H. Reeve: 'Remains of A. de Tocqueville', in *Edinburgh Review*, 1861. (Personal and eulogistic.)

   b. M. de Sacy: *Variétés littéraires* Tome II, Paris 1860.

   c. Lacordaire et Guizot: *Discours de réception à l'Académie Française*, 1861.

   d. Comte L. de Kergorlay: 'Etude littéraire sur M. de Tocqueville' (Mainly an appreciation of Tocqueville as a writer.)

   e. P. Janet: 'A. de Tocqueville', in *Revue des Deux Mondes* 1861. (A summary of his work, and a criticism of his methods.)

   f. L. de Loménie: 'Publicistes Modernes de la France: A. de Tocqueville', in *Revue des Deux Mondes*. (On Tocqueville as a political philosopher.)

   g. C. de Rémusat: 'De l'esprit de réaction: Royer-Collard et Tocqueville', in *Revue des Deux Mondes*, 1861. (Useful summary of Tocqueville's opinions in *De la Démocratie en Amérique*, but weak on his reaction to 1848.)

4. Reviews of the *Oeuvres Complètes*. (Not an exhaustive list.)

   a. Sainte-Beuve: 'Oeuvres et Correspondences Inédites de M. de Tocqueville', in *Causeries du Lundi*, Tome 15e, Paris 1862. (Good on Tocqueville's reaction to 1848: *'le théoricien était confondu et stupéfait'* [the theoretican was confused and dumbfounded], p. 114; also points out that

Tocqueville was a good analyst but had no solution for the problems of his generation.)

  b. *Pall Mall Gazette*, London 1865. Review of Vols VII and VIII of the *OE.C.* (The first to stress the inner conflict between heart and head.)

  c. *Pall Mall Gazette*, London 1865. Review of Vol. VIII of the *OE.C.* (By an admirer: calls him 'one of the noblest and wisest philosophic statesmen that ever lived', and gives high praise for his style.)

5. Miscellaneous

  a. *Le Moniteur*, 19th August 1836. Contains speech by M. Villemain on awarding prize to Tocqueville for first part of *De la Démocratie en Amérique*.

  b. Prévost-Paradol: *Essais de Politique et de Littérature* II, 1863. (An appreciation by a disappointed liberal.)

  c. Laboulage: *L'Etat et ses limites*, Paris 1860. (Contains references to Tocqueville's opinion on the powers of the state.)

**Note:** Not one of these authors had seen either the intimate correspondence, the document of 1841 [see A. Rédier, *Comme disait Monsieur de Tocqueville*, pp. 45–8] or the text of *Souvenirs*.

## b) 1870–1914

1. F. A. M. Mignet: *Nouveaux éloges historiques*, 1877. (Includes an essay on Tocqueville.)

2. Charles de Grandemaison: 'Tocqueville à Tours', published in *Le Correspondant* for April, 1879. (This gives information on the sources consulted by Tocqueville for *L'Ancien Régime*, and his method of note-taking.)

3. Jaques: *Alexis de Tocqueville*, Vienna 1876. (A useful summary of Tocqueville's opinions by a liberal.)

4. J. Bryce: *The predictions of Hamilton and de Tocqueville*, Johns Hopkins University studies in history and political science, H. B. Adams, editor, 5th series, No. 9, Baltimore 1887. (A useful summary of Tocqueville's predictions and a criticism of Tocqueville as a political philosopher.)

5. A. V. Dicey: 'Alexis de Tocqueville', published in *National Review* August 1893. (Draws attention to the waning interest in the great liberals: Mill, Tocqueville, Grote and Grey.)

6. E. D. Eichtal: *Alexis de Tocqueville et la démocratie libérale*, Paris 1897. (An interpretation by a liberal.)

7. H. B. Adams: *Jared Sparks and Alexis de Tocqueville*, Baltimore 1898. (Indispensable for sources of Tocqueville's opinions on the importance of local government.)

8. D. G. Gilman: 'A. de Tocqueville and his work on America', published in *Century Magazine*, September 1898. (A short essay by an admirer.

Also contains the opinions of Mr F. J. Lippitt on Tocqueville as a man. Mr Lippitt assisted Tocqueville in collecting notes on America. Mr Lippitt thought he was anti-democratic.)

9. E. Faguet: *Politiques et Moralistes du dix-neuvième siècle*, Paris 1900. (Faguet was an admirer—'*c'est un professeur de politique, très lumineux, très bien renseigné et de grande allure*' [A professor of politics, his writings are very luminous, very well informed and have a broad sweep], p. 114.)

10. R. P. Marcel: *Essai politique sur Alexis de Tocqueville*, Paris 1910. (Marcel was the first to consult the unpublished papers at Tocqueville, and he quoted extensively from these in his book.)

## c) 1915–1939

1. A. Rédier: *Comme disait M. de Tocqueville*, Paris 1925. (Rédier worked for 15 years on the unpublished papers at Tocqueville. He also unearthed two important documents, one on Tocqueville's creed and the other on Tocqueville's opinions on the restoration of the monarchy in France. Rédier's judgements are interesting, but they must appear odd to all but those few who are working for the royalist cause in France.)

2. Ruggiero: *The History of European Liberalism*, London 1927. Translated by R. G. Collingwood. (Very useful for the sources of Tocqueville's opinions, and his influence on liberal thought.)

3. D. Woodruff: 'Tocqueville in U.S.A.', published in *Dublin Review*, April 1928. (Some reflections on the decline of liberalism.)

4. H. Göring: *Tocqueville und die Demokratie*, München and Berlin, 1928. (A tribute to Tocqueville by a German liberal.)

5. R. Soltau: *French Political Thought in the 19th Century*, London 1931. (Tocqueville's opinions on the dangers of economic inequality.)

6. C. Cestre: 'A. de Tocqueville, témoin et juge de la civilisation Américaine', published in *Revue des Cours et Conférences*, 1932 to 1933. (Cestre agrees with Tocqueville on the value of religion as a restraint on conduct.)

7. H. J. Laski: 'Alexis de Tocqueville and Democracy', published in *The Social and Political Ideas of some Representative Thinkers of the Victorian Age*, edited by F. C. J. Hearnshaw, London 1933. (Professor Laski used the three main texts and the 'Memoir and Remains of A. de Tocqueville' for his material. Laski represents Tocqueville as a forerunner of Marx and makes no reference to his associations with the Right.)

8. Dr A. Salomon: *Autorität und Freiheit*, Zurich 1935. (This contains long selections from Tocqueville's writings to illustrate the judgements of Dr Salomon expressed in the introduction. It is the only work of its kind on Tocqueville in German.)

9. G. W. Pierson: *Tocqueville and Beaumont in America*, New York 1938. (This work is an invaluable account of the sources of Tocqueville's ideas in *De la Démocratie en Amérique*. The bibliography is the most exhaustive I have seen.)

10. J. P. Mayer: *Prophet of the Mass Age: A study of Alexis de Tocqueville*, London 1939. (Written to introduce Tocqueville to English readers. Herr Mayer used the material discovered by A. Rédier.)

## G. Other Material Consulted

1. W. Bagehot: *Literary Studies*, Everyman's Library, London 1911, 2 vols. (Appendix I in Vol. I contains Tocqueville's letters on Louis Napoleon's *coup d'état* of 1851.)

2. H. Balzac: *L'Envers de l'Histoire Contemporaine*, Ernest Flammarion, [Editeur], Paris. (Very useful for life in Paris during the reign of Louis Philippe.)

3. H. Balzac: *Le Député d'Arcis*, Ernest Flammarion, [Editeur], Paris. (Good for the opinions of the provincials on the issues of that time.)

4. P. B. de Barante: *La Vie Politique de M. Royer-Collard, ses discours et ses écrits. 2 tomes*, Paris 1861. (Useful for opinions of Collard.)

5. L. Blanc: *Histoire de Dix Ans, 1830–40, 12e édition*, Paris 1877.

6. A. Blanqui: '*Des classes ouvrières en France pendant l'année 1848*', published in *Petits Traités publiés par l'Académie des sciences morales et politiques*. Paris 1849. (Gives details of wages, living conditions etc. of working classes.)

7. L. G. A. de Bonald: *Les Vrais Principes opposés aux erreurs du XIXe siècle ou notions positives sur les points fondamentaux de la philosophie, de la politique et de la religion*, Avignon 1833. (A short statement of Catholic opinions—the philosophical creed of the 'Ultras'.)

8. F. R. de Chateaubriand: *Mémoires d'Outre-tombe*, Edition Nelson.

9. G. Flaubert: *L'Education Sentimentale*, Edition Nelson. (Depressing and sordid but invaluable for its descriptions of bourgeois society.)

10. F. Guizot: *Memoirs to illustrate the History of my Time*, 2 vols, London 1858, translated by J. W. Cole.

11. H. Heine: *Französische Zustände*, published in vols VIII to XI of the *Sämmtliche Werke*, Hamburg 1874.

12. V. Hugo: *Les Misérables*, 4 vols, Edition Nelson.

13. F. Jellinek: *Paris Commune of 1871*, London 1937.

14. A. de Lamartine: *Lectures pour Tous—Extraits des Oeuvres Générales de Lamartine, choisis par lui-même*, 2e édition, Paris 1855.

15. F. Lamennais: *Essai sur l'Indifférence en matière de réligion*, Edition Dent, London. (Gives the arguments for religion as a restraint upon human behaviour.)

16. F. G. Lamennais: *Paroles d'un Croyant*, Edition Dent, London.

17. F. Lamennais: *Lettres inédites de Lamennais à Montalembert*, Edited by E. Fargues, Paris 1898. (Religion and society.)

18. K. Marx: *The Class Struggles in France, 1848–50*, Martin Lawrence, London.

19. *The Eighteenth Brumaire of Louis Bonaparte*, Marxist Leninist Library, Moscow 1934.

20. K. Marx: *The Civil War in France*, Lawrence and Wishart, London.

21. Normanby, Marquis of: *A Year of Revolution from a journal kept in Paris in 1848*, 2 vols, London 1857. (Useful for the opinions and behaviour of the Party of Order, and for the influence of the British Government on Lamartine's Government.)

22. R. W. Postgate: *Revolution from 1789–1906*, Grant Richards, London 1920.

23. P. J. Proudhon: *Oeuvres Complètes de P.J. Proudhon*, Marpeu et Flammarion, éditeurs, Paris.

24. G. Sand: *Le Meunier d'Angibault*, Edition Nelson. (A novel on class relations in rural France; indicates the type attracted to socialism.)

25. H. A. Taine: *Les Origines de la France Contemporaine: La Révolution*, 2 tomes, Paris 1881.

26. G. Weill: *Histoire du Parti Républicain en France, 1814–70*, Paris 1928.

27. L. Woolf: *The Barbarians at the Gate*, London 1939.

# Chronology

| | |
|---|---|
| **15.8.1769** | Birth of Napoleon Bonaparte (Napoleon I) in Ajaccio, Corsica |
| **26.1.1788** | First Fleet lands 736 convicts at Port Jackson, New South Wales |
| **14.7.1789** | Storming of the Bastille in Paris |
| **3.9.1791** | National Assembly passes French Constitution |
| **21.1.1793** | Execution of King Louis XVI of France |
| **28.7.1794 [10 Thermidor]** | Fall of Robespierre |
| **3.11.1795** | Directory takes over Government of France |
| **9.11.1799 [18 Brumaire]** | *Coup d'état*: Consulate of three to govern France |
| **24.12.1799** | Napoleon Bonaparte becomes First Consul |
| **2.12.1804** | Napoleon I crowned Emperor in Notre Dame, Paris |
| **29.7.1805** | Birth of Alexis de Tocqueville |
| **20.4.1808** | Birth of Louis Napoleon Bonaparte (Napoleon III), nephew of Napoleon I |
| **11.4.1814** | Napoleon I abdicates and retires to Elba |
| **1814–1830** | Bourbon Restoration in France |
| **1814–1824** | Louis XVIII (Bourbon) |
| **29.5.1815** | Napoleon I takes Paris after return from Elba |
| **18.6.1815** | Napoleon I defeated at Waterloo |
| **5.5.1818** | Birth of Karl Marx |
| **5.5.1821** | Death of Napoleon I on St Helena |

| | |
|---|---|
| **30.10.1821** | Birth of Fyodor Dostoevsky |
| **16.9.1824** | Death of Louis XVIII, succeeded by his brother Charles X (Bourbon) |
| **4.7.1830** | Reactionary *coup d'état* by Charles X leads to revolution |
| **5.7.1830** | France annexes Algiers |
| **9.8.1830** | Louis Philippe d'Orléans elected King of the French |
| **1830–July 1848** | July Monarchy of Louis Philippe |
| **May 1831– February 1832** | Alexis de Tocqueville and Gustave de Beaumont travel in USA and Canada to study the penitentiary system |
| **1832** | Reform Bill in Britain extends franchise to about 500 000 electors |
| **January 1833** | Publication of report by Tocqueville and Beaumont on 'The Penitentiary System in the US and its Application in France', with an appendix, 'Penal Colonies', including an account of Australian Penal Colonies |
| **1834** | Abolition of slavery in British Empire |
| **1835** | Publication of *De la Démocratie en Amérique*, Part 1, by Tocqueville |
| **1840–46** | Louis Napoleon imprisoned in fortress at Ham after his attempted landing at Boulogne |
| **1840** | Publication of *De la Démocratie en Amérique*, Part 2 |
| **1.8.1840** | End of transportation of convicts from Britain to New South Wales |
| **1848** | Publication of *The Communist Manifesto* of Marx and Engels |
| | Abolition of slavery throughout French Empire |
| **24.2.1848** | Abdication of Louis Philippe |
| **27.2.1848** | National Workshops established in Paris by Provisional Government |
| **15.5.1848** | Communist rising in Paris |
| **23–26.6.1848** | Cavaignac suppresses National Workshops after June Days in Paris |
| **10.12.1848** | Louis Napoleon elected President of France |
| **13.6.1849** | Communist rising in Paris suppressed |
| **26.8.1850** | Death of Louis Philippe |

| | |
|---|---|
| **16.9.1850** | 16 000 people meet in Sydney to protest against renewal of transportation to the eastern colonies |
| **2.12.1851** | *Coup d'état* by Louis Napoleon |
| **21.12.1851** | New French constitution approved |
| **1852–1870** | Second Empire |
| **2.12.1852** | Louis Napoleon proclaimed Emperor of France as Napoleon III |
| **16.6.1856** | Publication of *L'Ancien Régime et la Révolution* by Tocqueville |
| **16.4.1859** | Death of Tocqueville in Cannes |
| **3.3.1861** | Emancipation decree for serfs in Russia |
| **1861–65** | Civil War in United States |
| **18.12.1865** | Abolition of slavery in United States by 13th Amendment to American Constitution |
| **10.1.1868** | Last convict ship to Australia, the *Hougoumont*, arrives in Western Australia |
| **1893** | Publication of Tocqueville's *Souvenirs* |

# Biographical
# and Topical Index

**Ampère, Jean-Jacques Antoine (1800–1864)**
French historian and philologist. Professor Univ. of Paris.
Works include *Histoire de la Poésie* (1830); *Promenade en Amérique* (1855).

**Bagehot, Walter (1826–1877)**
English economist and journalist. Editor of *The Economist*.
Works include *The English Constitution* (1867); *Physics and Politics* (1872); *Lombard Street* (1873); *Biographical Studies; Literary Studies.*

**Balzac, Honoré de (1799–1850)**
Came to Paris 1818, abandoned law to become editor, printer. Associate of V. Hugo, de Vigny, Lamartine, G. Sand. Founder of realist novel.
Novel Series: *La Comédie Humaine*, including *Le Père Goriot, Le Député d'Arcis.*

**Barante, Prosper Brugière, Baron de (1782–1866)**
French politician and historian.

**Barbès, Armand (1809–1870)**
Republican conspirator under July monarchy, one of the leaders of progressive party in 1848, elected to Constituent Assembly. Arrested as one of the principal instigators of the Communist rising of 15 May 1848, sentenced to life imprisonment but released in 1854.

**Baroche, Pierre Jules (1802–1870)**
Deputy in 1847. February 1848 signed demand to impeach Guizot and his ministry. Supported Barrot. Alarmed at socialist revolutionary agitation, supported the Party of Order. 1850 replaced Barrot as Minister for Interior and supported repressive measures. 1870 dissolved Assembly in face of German victories.

**Barrot, Odilon (1791–1873)**
Lawyer, liberal deputy under July monarchy, leader of 'dynastic left'. Active in banquets campaign February 1848. Member Constituent and Legislative Assemblies, formed his first ministry in December 1848. Retired from public life after *coup d'état* of 2 December 1851.

**Beaumont, Gustave de (1802–1866)**
Close friend of A. de Tocqueville, whom he accompanied in America. Deputy under the July monarchy ('dynastic left'), member of Constituent and Legislative Assemblies. Resigned as ambassador to Vienna after the *coup d'état* of December 1851 and left public life.

**Blanc, Louis (Jean Joseph Charles-Louis) (1811–1882)**
French socialist, journalist. Attacked policies and methods of Louis Philippe's government in *Histoire de dix ans 1830–1840* (1841–44). Member of the Provisional Government 1848, forcing Government to guarantee employment to workers. After failure of policy took refuge in England. Returned to France and elected to Chamber of Deputies 1871.
Work: *Histoire de la Révolution Française* (1847–62).

**Blanqui, Louis-Auguste (1805–1881)**
French socialist and revolutionary. Advocated insurrection by trained guerrilla groups and state socialism under temporary revolutionary dictatorship. Founded numerous secret societies. Took part in revolutions of 1830, 1848 and 1871 and insurrections in 1827, 1839, 1870. Spent more than 33 years in prison. President of Paris Commune in 1870.

**Boethius, Anicius Manlius Severinus (*c.* 480–524)**
Roman philosopher. His greatest work, *De Consolatione Philosophiae*, was written while he was in prison in Pavia for allegedly conspiring against the Emperor Theodoric.

**Bonald, Louis-Gabriel-Ambroise Vicomte de (1754–1840)**
French publicist and philosopher. An *émigré* during French Revolution. On his return to France, became a leader of Legitimists. Works include *Théorie du pouvoir politique et religieux* (1796).

**Bonaparte**
See Napoleon Bonaparte (1769–1821) and Napoleon III (1808–73)

**Carlists**
Carlism is a monarchical movement originating in Spain. In France the term 'Carlist' is applied to the supporters of Charles X and his descendants.

**Catiline, Lucius Sergius Catilina (*c.* 108–62 BC)**
Conspired twice unsuccessfully (in 65 and 62 BC) to attain power as Consul in Rome by murder and incendiarism.

**Cavaignac, Louis-Eugène (1802–1857)**
General in Africa under July monarchy. Minister for War 17 May 1848, given full powers in June 1848, crushed June insurrection. Arrested on 2 December 1851.

**Champ de Mars**
In Paris, scene of many historical events. On 17 July 1791 a petition demanding revolutionary changes was deposited on an altar there. A fusillade fired by the National Guard to disperse the crowd killed a number of people, leading to a split between moderate and radical revolutionaries.

**Charles X (1757–1836) of the House of Bourbon**
King of France 1824–30

**Chateaubriand, François-Auguste-René Vicomte de (1768–1848)**
French writer and statesman. Travelled in USA 1791–92, returned to France and fought in Royalist army 1792; *émigré* in England 1793–1800. Served under Napoleon I as minister to Valais, supported Bourbon cause 1814, Minister for Foreign Affairs 1823–24. Works include *Atala* (1801); *Le Génie du Christianisme* (1802); *Mémoires d'outre-tombe* (1849–50).

**Circourt, Anne-Marie-Joseph Albert Comte de (1809–1895)**
Conservative literary historian.

**'Cliveden Set'**
In the 1930s, a group of prominent British Conservatives including Neville Chamberlain and Sir Samuel Hoare were frequently enter-

tained at Cliveden, the country seat of Nancy Lady Astor (1879–1964), who succeeded her husband Waldorf Astor and became the first woman to sit in the British Parliament.

**Corcelles, Claude-François-Philibert-Tircuy de (1802–1892)**
Friend of Alexis de Tocqueville, Catholic Liberal in his youth, elected deputy in 1839, sat with the Liberals, opposed *coup d'état*, briefly imprisoned. Later re-organised Papal finances.

**Crawford, Raymond Maxwell (1906–1991)**
Professor of History, University of Melbourne 1937–70.

**Dicey, Albert Venn (1835–1922)**
English jurist, taught at Oxford and London. His *Lectures Introductory to the Study of the Law of the Constitution* (1885) are now considered part of the English Constitution.

**Dostoevsky, Fyodor Mikhailovich (1821–1881)**
Russian writer. Born in Moscow, served as officer in military engineering department. Retired early to write. Arrested and imprisoned in 1849 for participation in radical Petrashevsky circle. Reprieved from death sentence and transported to Siberia until 1854. His important metaphysical and psychological novels culminate in *The Brothers Karamazov* (1880).

**Flaubert, Gustave (1821–1880)**
French novelist. Pioneer and master of realist school of French literature. Prosecuted but acquitted of immorality after publication of *Madame Bovary* (1857). Later works include *L'Education Sentimentale* (1869).

**Fould, Achille-Marcus (1800–1867)**
Son of a banker, deputy from 1842, conservative voter, supported Guizot. After 1848 member of Constituent Assembly. Appointed Finance Minister by Louis Napoleon in 1849.

**Gobineau, Joseph-Arthur Comte de (1816–1882)**
French diplomat, orientalist and writer. Secretary to Alexis de Tocqueville in 1849. Best known for *Essai sur l'inégalité des races humaines* (1854–55) in which he advanced the theory of the superiority of the Aryan race.

**Grote, George (1794–1871)**
English historian. Member of circle of J. Bentham and J. S. Mill. MP 1832–41.

Works include *Essentials of Parliamentary Reform* (1831); *History of Greece* (1846–56).

### Guizot, François-Pierre-Guillaume (1787–1874)

French historian and politician. Professor in Paris in 1812. Advocated constitutional monarchy. Foreign Minister 1840–47. Premier of France 1847–48. Forced to retire by 1848 revolution.

Works include *Histoire de la Civilisation en Europe* (1828).

### Ham

French town on the Somme. The town's fortress was used as a State prison, in which Louis Napoleon was incarcerated 1840–46.

### Heine, Heinrich (1797–1856)

German lyric poet and sardonic political and social critic. Resident in Paris from 1831.

Works include *Buch der Lieder* (1827); *Französische Zustände* (1832–48).

### Hugo, Victor-Marie (1802–1885)

French writer. Leader of Romantic movement. Performance of his play *Hernani* caused stormy clashes between Classicists and Romantics. Granted pension by Louis XVIII. Member of Constituent Assembly. Banished from France by Napoleon III. Lived on Guernsey, where he wrote *Les Misérables*, until 1870.

### Hume, David (1711–1776)

Scottish philosopher and historian, known for his philosophical scepticism.

Works include *A Treatise of Human Nature* (1739–40); *Essays Moral and Political* (1741–42).

### Ingersoll, Charles Jared (1782–1862)

American lawyer and congressman, dramatist, historian. Born and died in Philadelphia, Jeffersonian Republican, then Jacksonian Democrat. In Congress 1813–15 and 1841–49.

### Jacobins

Political club founded in Versailles in 1789, later identified with supporters of radical centralist democracy.

### Kant, Immanuel (1724–1804)

German philosopher. Professor of Logic and Physics in Königsberg 1755–97. Influenced first by Leibniz, then by Hume and English empiricists; developed philosophy concerned with nature and limits of human knowledge and ethics.

Works include *Critik der reinen Vernunft* (1781); *Critik der practischen Vernunft* (1788).

### Kergorlay, Louis-Gabriel-César de (1804–1880)

A fervent legitimist. Refused to swear allegiance to Louis Philippe in 1830. Tocqueville's defence contributed to his release from prison in 1832. His correspondence with Tocqueville numbered some 200 letters.

### Lamartine, Alphonse de (1790–1869)

French poet and politician. Deputy under the July monarchy, opponent of Guizot, attended the 'banquets'. Minister for Foreign Affairs under Provisonal Government, overthrown in June 1848. Polled poorly in Presidential election and left public life after the *coup d'état* of 1851.

### Lamennais, Hughes Félicité Robert de (1782–1854)

French priest and philosopher. Defended Ultramontanism in 1814. Later changed his position and advocated alliance of Catholicism with political liberalism in the journal *L'Avenir*, which was suppressed in 1831. Denounced the Papacy and European monarchs in *Paroles d'un Croyant* (1834). Served in Constituent Assembly after 1848 revolution.

### Laski, Harold Joseph (1893–1950)

English political scientist. Professor of Political Science, London School of Economics. Chairman of British Labour Party 1945.

### Le Peletier de Rosanbo (?–1794)

Maternal grandfather of Alexis de Tocqueville. President of the court of the *Chambre des Vacations*. Arrested on 17 December 1793 at Malesherbes and executed on 20 April 1794 for complicity in a protest by the Parlement of Paris.

### Lewis, Sir George Cornwall (1806–1863)

British statesman and author. Classical scholar. Appointed to inquire into condition of poorer classes in Ireland, Midlands and Scotland. Elected as Liberal to House of Commons 1847. Chancellor of Exchequer 1855, later Home Secretary. Numerous wide-ranging publications.

### Louis Napoleon

See Napoleon III.

### Louis-Philippe (1773–1850) of the House of Orleans

King of the French 1830–48.

### Maistre, Joseph-Marie Comte de (1753–1821)

French polemical writer and diplomat. Emigrated to Switzerland 1792. Traditionalist.

Works include *Considérations sur la France* (1796).

### Malesherbes, Chrétien Guillaume de Lamoignon de (1721–1794)

French statesman. Defended King Louis XVI during his trial, for which he was executed in 1794. Maternal great-grandfather of Alexis de Tocqueville, who in *De la Démocratie en Amérique* quoted his address to King Louis XVI on centralisation.

### Mill, J. S. (1806–1873)

English philosopher and economist. A utilitarian in early life under influence of J. Bentham. MP 1865–68; voted with the advanced Radical party. Author of many works, including *On Liberty* (1859); *On the Subjection of Women* (1869).

### Montagnards

Under the Second Republic, this name was given to the deputies on the Left of the Constituent Assembly (1848). They campaigned for the right to work. The Party of Order took steps to eliminate them in 1850.

### Montalembert, Charles Forbes Comte de (1810–1870)

French politician and writer. Born in London, peer of France under July monarchy, elected to Constituent and Legislative Assemblies. Liberal Catholic associated with Lamennais and *L'Avenir*.

### Montesquieu, Charles de Secondat, Louis Baron de la Brède (1689–1755)

Lawyer at Bordeaux, then unattached man of letters. His main work was *De l'Esprit des Lois* (1750), published anonymously and placed on Catholic Index of forbidden works. The interpretation was relativist, praising the English constitution with its separation of powers. Contributed article on *'Goût'* (Taste) to the *Encyclopédie*.

### Napoleon Bonaparte (1769–1821)

Born in Ajaccio, Corsica. Reigned as Napoleon I, Emperor of the French 1804–13.

### Napoleon III Charles Louis Napoléon Bonaparte (1808–73)

Emperor 1851–70. Born in Paris, son of King Louis (Bonaparte) of Holland. Emulating his uncle, Napoleon I, he tried three times to recapture power before being elected president of the Second

Republic of France in 1848. In 1851, by a *coup d'état*, he became Emperor Napoleon III with absolute power. His empire was defeated by Prussia in 1870 and France was again declared a Republic.

**Pailleron, Edouard (1834–1899)**
French playwright and poet.
Works include *Le Monde où l'on s'amuse* (1868); *Le monde où l'on s'ennuie* (1881).

**Pirenne, Henri (1862–1935)**
Belgian historian, Professor at University of Ghent 1886–1930. Imprisoned by Germans 1916–18 for refusal to teach during their occupation of Belgium.
Works include *Histoire de Belgique* (1900–32); *Les anciennes démocraties des Pays-Bas* (1910).

**Proudhon, Pierre-Joseph (1809–1865)**
French journalist and socialist, 'father of anarchism'. Active in socialist movement in Paris 1848. Founded and edited radical journals such as *La Voix du Peuple* (1849–50). Famous for his slogans: 'Property is theft' and 'anarchy or Caesarism'. Imprisoned several times.
Greatest work: *Système des Contradictions Economiques* (1846).

**Radnor, Lord (Bouverie, William Pleydell, third Earl Radnor) (1779–1869)**
Whig politician, partly educated in France. Staunch advocate of popular rights, friend of William Cobbett.

**Reeve, Henry (1813–1895)**
Man of letters with cosmopolitan associations. Editor of the *Edinburgh Review* 1855–95. His English translation of Alexis de Tocqueville's *De la Démocratie en Amérique* appeared in 1835 (Part I) and 1840 (Part II).

**Rollin, Charles (1661–1741)**
French historian and educationist. Ardent Jansenist, Rector of *l'Université*.
Works include *Traité des Etudes; Histoire ancienne; Histoire romaine.*

**Royer-Collard, Pierre-Paul (1763–1845)**
French philosopher and politician. Secretary of Paris Commune 1790–92. A leader of the Doctrinaires after the Restoration;

advocate of constitutional monarchy, member (1815–42) and president (1828) of Chamber of Deputies. Developed a realist 'philosophy of perception'.

### Sand, George (1804–1876)
Pen name of Amandine-Aurore-Lucile Dudevant, née Dupin. French novelist. Began writing career in Paris, 1831. Noted for her championship of women and for liaisons with Prosper Mérimée, Alfred de Musset and Frédéric Chopin.
Works include *La Mare au Diable* (1846); *Le Meunier d'Angibault* (1845).

### Senior, Nassau William (1790–1864)
English economist. First professor of Political Economy, Oxford (1825–30, 1847–52).
Works include *An Outline of the Science of Political Economy* (1836).

### Shaw, Bernard (1856–1950)
Irish-born dramatist, critic, economic and political theorist.

### Sidney, Sir Philip (1554–1586)
English soldier, statesman and poet.
Works include *Arcadia* (sonnets); *The Defense of Poesie; Astrophel and Stella*.

### Sparks, Jared (1789–1866)
American historian. Born Wilmington, Connecticut. Edited *North American Review* 1823–29. Published many works on the American Revolution. Professor at Harvard University 1839–49.

### Stoffels, Eugène, Baron (1821–1907)
Army officer, served in campaign against Austria, supported Napoleon III. Closest friend of A. de Tocqueville.

### Sumner, Benedict Humphrey (1893–1951)
Educated at Winchester, don at Balliol College Oxford (1912–14, 1922–44), All Souls' (1945–51).
Works include *Russia and the Balkans* (1937); *Survey of Russian History* (1945); *Peter the Great and the Ottoman Empire* (1941); *Peter the Great and the Emergence of Russia* (1950).

### Swetchine, Madame Anne Sophie, née Soymanov (1782–1857)
Born Moscow, married General Swetchine, converted to Catholicism 1815, moved to Paris, maintained a salon marked by courtesy, intellectual brilliance, religious feeling and mysticism.
Works include *Old Age; Resignation*.

**Taine, Hippolyte-Adolphe (1828–1893)**
French philosopher, historian and critic. Leading French Positivist. Professor at Ecole des Beaux-Arts, Paris 1864–84.
Main work: *Origines de la France contemporaine* (1876–99).

**Thackeray, William Makepeace (1811–1863)**
English novelist. Entered Middle Temple but turned to journalism. Contributed fiction regularly to *Fraser's Magazine* and *Punch*.
Works include *Vanity Fair* (1847–50); *Henry Esmond* (1852).

**Thiers, Louis-Adolphe (1797–1877)**
French politician and historian. Minister (1832, 1834–36) and Premier (1836, 1840) under Louis Philippe. A moderate in revolution of 1848, banished 1851–52. Leader of opposition under Napoleon III. Crushed Paris Commune 1871.
Main work: *Histoire de la révolution française* (1823–27).

**Ultramontanes**
In the nineteenth century this name was given to those who resisted attempts to subordinate Church to State.

**Vichy**
Best-known spa in France. After the defeat of the French armies by the Axis Powers in June 1940, Marshal Pétain's French puppet government was located in Vichy until 1943.

**Vigny, Alfred-Victor Comte de (1797–1863)**
Officer in French army 1814–26. Leader of French Romantics.
Works include *Poèmes* (1822); *Servitude et Grandeur militaires* (1835).

**Winthrop, John (1587–1649)**
Born in Suffolk, England. Practised as a lawyer in London. Sailed to Massachusetts in 1630 as elected Governor of Puritan colonists. He disliked political democracy and believed in a 'spiritual aristocracy'. In *De la Démocratie en Amérique,* Tocqueville gives as a definition of liberty a freely translated passage from John Winthrop's famous speech of 1645, as reported in Cotton Mather, *Magnalia Christi Americana* (1702).

**Woolf, Leonard Sidney (1880–1969)**
English historian and political essayist.
Works include *After the Deluge* (1931); *Barbarians at the Gate* (1939).

# Tocqueville
# and the Translations

To satisfy a curiosity about Tocqueville and his thought, most Australians must be content with translations of his major works and of a biography,[1] plus the multitudinous commentaries, each of which, as Manning Clark points out in his thesis, tends to set Tocqueville's message to its own particular tune.

No one is more conscious of the limitations of translation than a conscientious translator. Tocqueville's prose brings one face-to-face with these limitations in almost every line. His political and historical language is not a clotted polysyllabic jargon but luminous with images and striking antitheses. It expresses, often in words of one syllable, the idealism and passion of a very sensitive mind.

One of these simple words of one syllable has caused Tocqueville's translators a deal of trouble: *goût*, which, as we know, means taste. But what are we to make of *le goût sublime de la liberté* or *un goût de tête pour la démocratie*, or *un goût dépravé pour l'égalité*? The word 'taste' seems incongruous in these contexts. Perplexed translators have substituted for it variously: 'inclination', 'affection', 'predilection', 'preference' and other locutions. Perhaps, after all, it is best to keep the word 'taste', trusting the reader to make a linguistic leap and invest the word with the author's shades of meaning.

This intended meaning is illustrated in a passage from an extraordinary 'confession' or self-examination by Tocqueville, discovered by A. Rédier[2] and quoted by Clark on pages 74–5:

---

[1] André Jardin, *Tocqueville—A Biography*, 1988.
[2] A. Rédier, *Tocqueville*, pp. 46–8.

*J'ai pour les institutions démocratiques un goût de tête, mais je suis aristocratique par l'instinct . . . La liberté est la première de mes passions. Voilà ce qui est vrai.*

[I have an intellectual taste for democratic institutions, but I am aristocratic by instinct ... Liberty is the foremost of my passions. And that is the truth of the matter.]

Where Tocqueville's warm and instinctive feelings are engaged, we usually find the word *passion*. The word *goût* generally indicates a lower attachment—sometimes intellectual like *un goût de tête*, sometimes equivocal or even unworthy, as in *un goût dépravé pour l'égalité*.

This last phrase occurs in *De la Démocratie en Amérique* in a paragraph discussing equality:

*Il y a . . . <u>une passion mâle et légitime pour l'égalité</u> qui . . . tend élever les petits au rang des grands; mais il se rencontre aussi dans le coeur humain <u>un goût dépravé pour l'égalité</u>, qui . . . réduit les hommes à préférer l'égalité dans la servitude à l'iné- galité dans la liberté.*

[There is a manly and legitimate passion for equality which tends to raise little men to the level of the great. But the human heart can also harbour a depraved taste for equality which reduces men to preferring equality in servitude to inequality in freedom.][3]

As an example of what might be called tendentious quotation, we should note here that in his thesis Clark refers a number of times to what Tocqueville stigmatises as 'a depraved taste for equality', but never once to what he endorses as the 'manly and legitimate passion for equality'.

We have spoken of the perils of tendentious quotation and trans- lation. Even basic transcription can be tendentious. For Tocqueville, of all the great ideas which 'float before his eyes', surely liberty is the most crucial. Liberty is *'le premier des biens'*—'the greatest of all goods',[4] 'the first of the blessings'.[5] We must know what he

---

[3] A. de Tocqueville, *OE.C.* (1868 edition), vol. I, p. 86.

[4] J. Lively, *The Social and Political Thought of Alexis de Tocqueville*, Oxford, Clarendon Press, 1962, p. 20.

[5] J. P. Mayer, *Prophet of the Mass Age: a Study of Alexis de Tocqueville*, London, pp. 2, 126.

means by it. All interpreters of Tocqueville's work must come to grips with this, although not all have attempted to define *his* liberty. Even a cursory survey reveals a variegated tapestry.

Manning Clark himself states categorically in his thesis that Tocqueville made only two attempts to define his conception of liberty. The first, in 'the words of another man', was a purported quotation taken from a famous speech made in 1645 by John Winthrop, then Deputy Governor of the Puritan colony of Massachusetts. The second was a statement appearing in Tocqueville's *L'Ancien Régime*.[6]

Here is the relevant passage from Winthrop's speech as recorded in Cotton Mather's *Magnalia Christi Americana* (1702):

> Nor would I have you to mistake in the point of your own liberty. There is a liberty of corrupt nature which is affected both by men and beasts, to do what they list; and this liberty is inconsistent with authority, impatient of all restraint; by this liberty, *Sumus omnes Deteriores*; 'tis the grand enemy of truth and peace and all the Ordinances of God are bent against it. But there is a civil, a moral, a federal liberty, which is the proper end and object of authority; it is a liberty for that only which is just and good; for this liberty you are to stand with the hazard of your very lives.[7]

Now follows Tocqueville's translation of this passage, which he sets within quotation marks. Here and in succeeding extracts, ideas and expressions which do not occur in the original are underlined:

> *Ne* nous *trompons pas sur ce que* nous *devons entendre par* notre indépendance. *Il y a une sorte de liberté corrompue, dont l'usage est commun aux animaux comme à l'homme, et consiste à faire* tout *ce qui* plaît. *Cette liberté est* l'ennemie *de toute autorité. Elle souffre impatiemment toutes* règles; *avec elle, nous* devenons *inférieurs* à nous-mêmes; *elle est l'ennemie de la vérité et de la paix; et Dieu a* cru devoir s'élever contre elle! *Mais il est une liberté civile et morale* qui trouve sa force dans l'union, *et que la* mission *du* pouvoir lui-même *est de* pro-

---

[6] A. de Tocqueville, *OE.C.* (1868 edition), vol. I, p. 67.

[7] Cotton Mather, ed., *Magnalia Christi Americana, OR, the History of New England*, pp. 116–17. The same speech, in a slightly extended version, is also recorded in *The History of New England from 1630–1649* by John Winthrop, ed. James Savage, vols I and II, Arno Press, New York, 1972, vol. II, p. 229.

*téger: c'est la liberté <u>de faire sans crainte tout</u> ce qui est juste et bon. Cette <u>sainte</u> liberté <u>nous</u> devons la défendre <u>dans tous les hasards</u>, et exposer, <u>s'il le faut</u>, pour elle <u>notre</u> vie.*[8]

[Let <u>us</u> make no mistake about what <u>we</u> are to understand by <u>our independence</u>. There is in fact a <u>kind</u> of corrupt liberty, the practice of which is common to both animals and man, which consists of doing <u>everything</u> that <u>pleases</u>. This liberty is the enemy of all authority. It is impatient of all <u>rules.</u> By [exercising] this liberty, we <u>become</u> inferior <u>to ourselves</u>; it is the enemy of truth and peace; and God <u>believed it to be his duty to rise up against it</u>! But there is a civil and moral liberty <u>which finds its strength in the union</u>, and which it is the <u>mission</u> of the power [of the state] <u>to protect</u>. This is the liberty <u>to do without fear everything</u> that is just and good. It is <u>our</u> duty to defend this <u>sainted</u> liberty <u>against all hazards</u>, and, <u>if need be</u>, to risk <u>our</u> lives for it.]

In this version the Puritan severities, the commands 'you are to' and the references to the Ordinances of God have been softened to 'we are to' and notions of protection. The ideas of a 'holy' or 'sainted' liberty, and of practising virtue 'without fear' have been introduced—from nowhere.

In his thesis, Clark simply quotes Tocqueville, in quotation marks, as stating that 'Liberty is to do what is good and just "without compulsion"'. In his footnote, by misplacing a quotation mark, he actually attributes to Tocqueville approving comments which were in reality part of Winthrop's speech. Clark also makes his own 'creative' contribution to the definition: for Tocqueville's qualifying phrase 'without fear' he substitutes the much stronger 'without compulsion', which then becomes a key expression throughout the thesis. Clark's slips in dealing with this definition, however, may be excused by the difficult conditions under which he was working: his isolation and the inaccessibility of all source material.

But what are we to make of the creative leap of yet another 'transcription' of this famous passage of Winthrop's speech? This time it is quoted by the eminent American Chief Justice John Marshall (1755–1835) and occurs in his biography of George Washington. Tocqueville himself draws attention to it in a footnote. Once again enclosed in quotation marks, we read:

---

[8]  A. de Tocqueville, *OE.C.*, vol. I, p. 67.

There is a freedom of doing what we list, without regard to law or <u>justice:</u> this liberty is indeed inconsistent with authority; but civil, moral federal liberty <u>consists in every man enjoying his property, and having the benefit of the Laws of his country; which is very consistent with a due subjection to the civil magistrate.</u> And for this you ought to contend with the hazard of your lives.[9]

In what sense could this be called a 'quotation' from Winthrop's speech?

The second of Tocqueville's definitions of liberty, as recorded in the Clark thesis, occurs in *L'Ancien Régime*:

> . . . *c'est le plaisir de pouvoir parler, agir, respirer sans contrainte, sous le seul gouvernement de Dieu et les lois.*

> [. . . it is the pleasure of being able to speak, act and breathe without constraint, governed only by God and the laws.][10]

The definition is notable for its emotive language, its poetic expression. It is also remarkable for its rider: 'governed only by God and the laws', naming two concepts which themselves seem to cry out for definition. But for our purpose the significant word is '*contrainte*' (constraint). Clark fastens on to this word in three ways. Firstly, he gives the word its stronger meaning, compulsion. Secondly, he (consciously or unconsciously) substitutes it for '*crainte*' [fear] inserted by Tocqueville into the Winthrop definition. And thirdly, the words 'without compulsion' become a key phrase throughout the thesis. All this is well within the tradition of 'creative' transcription, translation and quotation practised by Tocqueville himself and many other distinguished writers, and by some of Tocqueville's interpreters.

Let us glance at a very few of the comments made by other writers on Tocqueville's conception of liberty. Many commentators appear to find it entirely unnecessary to examine what Tocqueville meant by the word. Irving M. Zeitlin, in his interesting analysis of Tocqueville's work, maintains that 'liberty is another key term Tocqueville chose never to define'.[11] Generally speaking, the Winthrop definition is totally ignored by commentators. Starting with Henry Reeve in

---

[9] J. Marshall, *The Life of Washington*, vol. I, pp. 145–6.
[10] A. de Tocqueville, *L'Ancien Régime*, p. 279.
[11] I. Zeitlin, *Liberty, Equality and Revolution in Alexis de Tocqueville*, p. 6. See also A. Rédier, *Tocqueville*, p. 78.

1835, translators into English of *De la Démocratie en Amérique* likewise ignore Tocqueville's version of this and simply quote the extract from John Winthrop's speech (literally or in paraphrase) direct from *Magnalia Christi Americana*.

That leaves us with the second 'definition' taken from *L'Ancien Régime*. If we examine the syntax of the passage in which this occurs we may in fact come to agree with Zeitlin that Tocqueville 'chose never to define' liberty itself, for this sentence seems to constitute a definition of liberty's 'intrinsic attractions, its own charm' rather than of the content of liberty itself. The paragraph reads:

> *Ce qui, dans tous les temps, lui [that is, à la liberté] a attaché si fortement le coeur de certains hommes, ce sont ses attraits mêmes, son charme propre, indépendant de ses bienfaits; c'est le plaisir de pouvoir parler, agir, respirer sans contrainte, sous le seul gouvernement de Dieu et les lois. Qui cherche dans la liberté autre chose qu'elle-même est fait pour servir.*[12]

> [What has, in all ages, so firmly attached the hearts of some men to it [that is, liberty] is <u>its intrinsic attractions, its own charm</u>, independent of its benefits; <u>it is the pleasure</u> of speaking, acting, breathing without constraint, governed only by God and the laws. He who seeks in liberty anything other than itself is fit only to serve.]

If we turn to Jack Lively's much-quoted work on Tocqueville, in his 21-page-long chapter headed 'Liberty', he concedes that Tocqueville 'never himself explicitly defined the content of liberty'.[13] He further draws on the paragraph just quoted from *L'Ancien Régime* to cite Tocqueville's belief that 'liberty must be sought as an end in itself, men must feel as necessary to their nature *the wish* 'to speak, act and breathe without restraint'.[14] But note that Lively omits entirely the all-important rider, 'governed only by God and the laws'. In fact, the religious elements of Tocqueville's 'passion for liberty' are totally ignored by Lively. He translates Tocqueville's adjective '*sainte*' as 'sacred' rather than 'holy' or 'sainted' and relates it entirely to the issue of man's freedom of choice.[15]

---

[12] A. de Tocqueville, *L'Ancien Régime*, p. 279. Cf. A. Rédier, *Tocqueville*, p. 159 (letter from Tocqueville to his wife, Marie Mottley).
[13] J. Lively, *Social and Political Thought*, p. 10.
[14] Ibid., p. 14.
[15] Ibid., p. 8.

This tendency to secularise Tocqueville's thought is common to many interpreters, but not to all. One wonders whether Lively can possibly be writing about the same man as Antoine Rédier, the author of the pioneering biography *Comme disait M. de Tocqueville*. In his chapter on *'La Liberté'*, Rédier writes that with the coming of Christ:

> All forms of servitude were abolished save one: On condition that he obeyed God, every man enjoyed sovereign freedom in his relations with his fellow-men . . .[16] Read Tocqueville. His conception of liberty was almost the same as that of these Christians . . .[17]

For Tocqueville, liberty has a single name, virtue:[18]

> Not holding any firm doctrine as regards liberty but only a loving sentiment, . . . like all lovers, where his love was concerned he no longer *thought*, he simply *sang*.[19]

Rédier also quotes Tocqueville:

> My greatest dream on entering politics was to work towards reconciling the liberal spirit with the spirit of religion, the new society with the Church.[20]

—and many similar passages.

Of other commentaries, there are two which give full and accurate accounts of Tocqueville's reflections on liberty, as expressed in *L'Ancien Régime*. The first, by J. P. Mayer, written on the eve of World War II, maintains that in these pages Tocqueville has indeed defined the nature of freedom, and that 'No one before him described more incisively the danger of freedom's eclipse'.[21]

The second is found in the last chapter of Hugh Brogan's short study, *Tocqueville*. It concludes with a catalogue of his shortcomings, including'

> an almost total disregard of the trifling grievances, such as disease, starvation and unemployment that occupied lesser mortals. None of this matters . . . there must still be many who,

---

[16] Rédier, *Tocqueville*, p. 53.
[17] Ibid., p. 54.
[18] Ibid., p. 60.
[19] Ibid., p. 148.
[20] Ibid., p. 55.
[21] Mayer, *Prophet of the Mass Age*, p. 134.

knowing Tocqueville's shortcomings, nevertheless believe, like
him, that the flame of liberty cannot and should not ever be put
out; who still see it as indispensable for the attainment of full
human stature . . .[22]

Tocquevilliana continues to be an area generating lively, global
debate. If the implications appear to be gloomy for those who intend
to study Tocqueville in translation, we should nevertheless take
heart. Our whole Western culture depends largely on the translations from Hebrew, Ancient Greek and Aramaic that constitute
the Christian Bible—and on ideas taken from translations of Ancient
Roman and Greek writers. Are not most English-speaking Marxists,
Freudians and many other idealists dependent on translations from
very convoluted German and other European and far-Eastern texts?
The serious reader of today is confronted by innumerable translations
of important texts from the various languages of every continent.

One thing remains certain. A serious interest in Tocqueville and
his thought is best served by studying his works as he himself wrote
them.

---

[22] H. Brogan, *Tocqueville*, p. 93.

# Bibliography

Auden, W. H. *Collected Shorter Poems 1930–1944*. Faber and Faber Ltd, London, 1950.

Berlin, Isaiah. *Four Essays on Liberty*. Oxford University Press, Oxford, 1979.

Bridge, Carl, ed. *Manning Clark—Essays on his Place in History*. Melbourne University Press, Carlton South, 1994.

Brogan, Hugh. *Tocqueville*. The Chaucer Press, Great Britain, 1973.

Bryce, James. *The American Commonwealth*. Macmillan, London, 1888.

Clark, C. M. H. *A History of Australia*, Vol. II, 'New South Wales and Van Diemen's Land', 1822–1838. Melbourne University Press, Carlton South, 1968.

—— *A History of Australia*, Vol. IV, 'The Earth Abideth Forever', 1851–1888. Melbourne University Press, Carlton South, 1978.

—— *A History of Australia*, Vol. V, 'The People Make Laws', 1888–1915. Melbourne University Press, Carlton South, 1981.

—— *A History of Australia*, Vol. VI, 'The Old Dead Tree and the Young Tree Green', 1916–1935. Melbourne University Press, Carlton South, 1987.

Clark, Manning. *Occasional Writings and Speeches*. Fontana/Collins, Melbourne, 1980.

—— *The Quest for Grace*. Penguin Books Australia, 1990.

—— *A Discovery of Australia*. ABC Enterprises, Crows Nest, 1991.

—— *A Historian's Apprenticeship*. Melbourne University Press, Carlton South, 1992.

—— *Speaking Out of Turn—Lectures and Speeches 1940–1991.* Melbourne University Press, Carlton South, 1997.

Crawford, R. M., Manning Clark and Geoffrey Blainey. *Making History.* McPhee Gribble/Penguin Books, Fitzroy, 1985.

Crook, David Paul. *American Democracy in English Politics 1815–1850.* Clarendon Press, London, 1965.

Deakin, Alfred. *The Federal Story: The Inner History of the Federal Cause 1880–1900.* Robertson & Mullens, Melbourne, 1944.

Dixson, Miriam. 'Clark and National Identity'. Carl Bridge (ed.). *Manning Clark—Essays on his Place in History*, pp. 188–206.

Forster, Colin. *France and Botany Bay—the Lure of a Penal Colony.* Melbourne University Press, Carlton South, 1996.

Headon, David, and Elizabeth Perkins, eds. *Our First Republicans: Selected Writings of John Dunmore Lang, Charles Harpur and Daniel Henry Deniehy 1840–1860.* The Federation Press, Sydney, 1998.

Holt, Stephen. *A Short History of Manning Clark.* Allen & Unwin, St Leonards (New South Wales), 1999.

Jardin, André. *Tocqueville—A Biography.* Peter Halban, London, 1988.

La Nauze, J. A. *The Making of the Australian Constitution.* Melbourne University Press, Carlton South, 1972.

Lawson, Henry. *Complete Works 1885–1900.* Vol. I. 'A Camp-Fire Yarn'. Leonard Cronin (ed.). Lansdowne, Sydney, 1984.

Macintyre, Stuart. 'Always a pace or two apart'. Carl Bridge (ed.). *Manning Clark—Essays on his Place in History*, pp. 17–29.

McLachlan, N. D. '"The Future America": Some Bicentennial Reflections'. *Historical Studies*, vol. 17, April 1977, pp. 361–83.

McQueen, Humphrey. *Suspect History.* Wakefield Press, Kent Town (South Australia), 1997.

Marshall, John. *The Life of George Washington.* 5 vols. Wayne, Philadelphia, 1804–1807.

Mather, Cotton. *Magnalia Christi Americana* [Book II] *or, The History of New England.* Hartford, 1820.

Mayer, J. P. *Prophet of the Mass Age: A study of Alexis de Tocqueville.* J. M. Dent and Sons Ltd, London, 1939.

Melbourne, A. C. V. *William Charles Wentworth.* Briggs, Brisbane, 1934.

*Official Report of the National Australasian Convention Debates.* George Stephen Chapman, Acting Government Printer, Sydney, 1891.

Rédier, Antoine. *Comme disait Monsieur de Tocqueville*. Perrin et Cie, Paris, 1925.

Rickard, John. 'Clark and Patrick White'. Carl Bridge (ed.). *Manning Clark—Essays on his Place in History*, pp. 45–54.

Ryan, Peter. 'Manning Clark'. *Quadrant.*, vol. 37, no. 9, 1993, pp. 9–22.

Shaw, G. P. 'A Sentimental Humanist'. Carl Bridge (ed.). *Manning Clark—Essays on his Place in History*, pp. 30–44.

Silvester, Edward Kennedy. *New South Wales Constitution Bill—The Speeches in the Legislative Council of New South Wales on the Second Reading of the Bill for Framing a New Constitution for the Colony of New South Wales*. Thomas Daniel, Sydney, 1853.

Tocqueville, Alexis de. *Oeuvres Complètes*. 9 vols. Gustave de Beaumont (ed.). Paris, 1868.

—— *Oeuvres Complètes*. Gallimard, Paris, 1951–.

—— *L'Ancien Régime et la Révolution*. Deuxième Edition. Lévy Frères, 1856.

Tocqueville, Alexis de. *Ecrits sur le Système Pénitentiaire en France et à l'Etranger*. [*Oeuvres Complètes*. Tome IV (1984). Gallimard, 1951–.]

Warden, James. 'Federalism and the Design of the Australian Constitution'. *Australian Journal of Political Science*, vol. 27, 1992, pp. 143–58.

Warhurst, John. 'In the Public Arena'. Carl Bridge (ed.). *Manning Clark—Essays on his Place in History*, pp. 153–64.

Winthrop, John. *The History of New England from 1630–1649*. Vols I and II. James Savage (ed.). Arno Press, New York, 1972.

Zeitlin, Irving. *Liberty, Equality and Revolution in Alexis de Tocqueville*. Little, Brown, Boston, 1971.

## Manuscript Sources

Manning Clark File, University of Melbourne Archives

Papers of Prof. C. M. H. Clark, National Library of Australia

Papers of Prof. R. M. Crawford, University of Melbourne Archives

# *Index*

**183**